The Foreign Language Teach

AIMING FOR PROFICIENCY

IN

SPANISH

Patricia A. Lennon
Douglas E. Moore
Rosemary L. Haigh
Carmela Taliercio

Language Consultants:

Margaret Fernández
John Christianson
Luz Castillo
Shannon Behrens
Stephanie O. Lunati
Madeline Turan
Eveny Pagán

ISBN 1-879279-26-6

Proficiency Press Co.

Foreign Language Books by Master Teachers for Master Teachers

Cover design by B. Soll Design, Inc.

OTHER BOOKS BY PROFICIENCY PRESS

The NEW Teacher's Handbook: Aiming for Proficiency in French
Teacher's Handbook: Aiming for Proficiency in German
Teacher's Handbook: Aiming for Proficiency in Italian
Teacher Handbook: Aiming for Proficiency in Spanish
Portfolio Assessment Tasks for the Beginning Level (All Languages)
Authentic Assessment for the Intermediate Level in Spanish
Authentic Assessment for the Intermediate Level in French
C'est Ton Tour, Aiming for Proficiency in French
Du Bist Dran, Aiming for Proficiency in German
Te Toca a Ti, Aiming for Proficiency in Spanish
Te Toca a Ti, Audio Cassette in Spanish
Tocca a Te, Aiming for Proficiency in Italian
It's Your Turn to Speak English (ESL)
¡Hola Soy Yo!
Ciao! Sono Io!
Salut! C'est Moi!
Suivez-Moi, Aiming for Proficiency in French
Seguimi, Aiming for Proficiency in Italian
Sígueme, Aiming for Proficiency in Spanish
Internet Tasks for Second Language Students (All Languages)
The Teacher's Guide for the Updated NYS Foreign Language
Proficiency Exam

First edition,   October 1989   Second through tenth printings, 1990-2001
Second edition,   September, 2002

The Foreign Language Teacher's Handbook:
AIMING FOR PROFICIENCY IN SPANISH

"This ready-to-use proficiency testing and authentic assessment book really makes teaching easier. The Teacher's Handbook is an extremely valuable professional resource for teachers who are implementing the National Standards."
> Marianne Scimeca, Bilingual Coordinator and Foreign Language Teacher
> East Grand Rapids School District

"AIMING FOR PROFICIENCY… serves as an excellent guidepost for teaching proficiency. A highly professional and much needed tool for teachers."
> Nancy McMahon, Past President
> NYS Association of Foreign Language Teachers

"Right on target!…the whole picture of the proficiency Exam is there. The first practical guide to come along in a long time."
> Gene Lowenberg, President
> American Association of Teachers of French
> Nassau County Chapter, L.I.

"You have a hit on your hands…as comprehensive a book as one can expect or needs to fulfill the requirements for Checkpoint A; also excellent for Checkpoints B and C. This is a well-produced, efficient book which should satisfy everyone."
> Joseph A. Tursi, Director of Arts
> in Foreign Language Teaching & of
> The Foreign Language Teacher Training Program
> SUNY Stony Brook

"At last, a guide for the classroom teacher which integrates topical vocabulary, pre-test activities, and communicative proficiency exams for Checkpoint A, including listening and speaking components."
> Adrienne Greenbaum,
> Language Coordinator
> Central Islip Schools

"Everything in the book matches the format of the Proficiency Exam. Students who use this book will be well prepared for the exam. This book can be used at all levels. Thank you for a fine book."
> Joan L. Feindler,
> Curriculum Associate for Foreign Languages
> East Williston Schools

ABOUT THE AUTHORS

Mrs. Rosemary Haigh (BA and MA in French, St. John's University; Fulbright Scholar; French Government Assistantship; graduate work at the Sorbonne, Paris; American Association of Teachers of French "National Secondary Teacher of the Year"; National Honoree in the "Walt Disney Salute to the American Teacher Program"). Mrs. Haigh has taught in France, Poland, Australia, and in the Sewanhaka Central High School District, where she was honored as "Teacher of the Year." Mrs. Haigh is certified to teach French from the pre-K through the advanced placement levels. She co-authored Sewanhaka Central High School District's *Curriculum Guides for French* as well as Proficiency Press Co publications: *C'est Ton Tour, The Teacher's Handbook in French, Suivez-Moi,* and *Authentic Assessment for the Intermediate Level.* Mrs. Haigh is a workshop presenter on the National Standards and on increasing French enrollment. She is an active member of AATF, ACTFL, NYSAFLT and LILT.

Mr. Richard B. Gentile (BA in French, State University of New York at Stony Brook; MA in French, St. John's University; Certificat d'Etudes Françaises, Université de Neuchâtel, Switzerland; graduate work at El Instituto de Cultura Hispánica, Spain; and the Université de Neuchâtel, Switzerland.) Mr. Gentile recently retired from Hicksville High School as a teacher of French, Spanish and English, and as an adjunct lecturer in French at Adelphi University. Mr. Gentile has had original French poetry published in *Poésie USA*, has co-authored the first complete English translation of George Sand's autobiography, *Story of My Life*, and has co-authored Proficiency Press' *Suivez-Moi* and *Authentic Assessment for the Intermediate Level in French.* He frequently presents workshops on the pedagogical values of the Internet. Mr. Gentile is an active member of AATF, LILT (co-founder and past president) and NYSAFLT.

Ms. Patricia A. Lennon (BA in Spanish, Molloy College; MA in Spanish, St. John's University; "Teacher of the Year," Sewanhaka High School District; two AATSP scholarships; finalist as "Teacher of the Year for New York State"; Embassy of Spain Scholarship, Salamanca, Spain) Ms. Lennon is a teacher of Spanish, ESL, and is Chairperson of Foreign Languages at Elmont Memorial High School. She co-authored Sewanhaka Central High School District's *Curriculum Guides for Spanish* and co-authored Proficiency Press publications: *The Teacher's Handbook in Spanish, Te Toca A Ti, Portfolio Assessment for the Beginning Level, Sígueme, Authentic Assessment for the Intermediate Level,* and *It's Your Turn To Speak English.* Ms. Lennon is a presenter of workshops on language proficiency, methodology and authentic assessment. She is an adjunct lecturer at Adelphi University. She is a member of the AATSP (Past President of the Long Island Chapter and past Newsletter editor), LILT and NYSAFLT.

Mr. Douglas E. Moore (BA in Spanish, MA in Teaching of English as a Second Language, Queens College, and has studied at the University of Valencia, Spain) has co-authored *Curriculum Guides* for the Sewanhaka District and piloted *The Exploratory Language Program in Spanish and French* for Jericho Public Schools. He has co-authored *The Teacher's Handbook in Spanish, Portfolio Assessment, Te Toca a Ti, Sígueme, Authentic Assessment for the Intermediate Level,* and *Internet Tasks for Second Language Students.* In addition, he has presented numerous workshops on communicative techniques and on the Internet. Mr. Moore currently teaches junior and senior high school Spanish in the South Huntington School District. He also teaches Spanish at Suffolk Community College and ESL at BOCES in Nassau County. He is an active member of NYSAFLT, LILT and AATSP (past treasurer).

Mrs. Carmela Taliercio-Cohn (BA in Italian, St. John's University; MA in Italian, Middlebury College, Middlebury School in Florence, University of Florence; AATI Travel/Study Grant, Perugia, Italy.) Mrs. Taliercio-Cohn is a native of two cultures, having attended elementary and undergraduate schools in the United States and secondary and graduate schools in Italy. Mrs. Taliercio-Cohn thus brings a unique and modern perspective to her teaching and her writing. As a teacher of Italian at Elmont Memorial High School in the Sewanhaka Central High School District, she authored *Curriculum Guides in Italian for Checkpoints A and B*. She is also an active member of AATI and NYSAFLT. Mrs. Taliercio-Cohn presents workshops on foreign language proficiency and on the Internet. In addition, Mrs. Taliercio-Cohn co-authored the following Proficiency Press publications: *The Teacher's Handbook in Italian, Tocca a Te, Seguimi;* and *Internet Tasks for Second Language Students.*

INTRODUCTION

The Foreign Language Teacher's Handbook:
AIMING FOR PROFICIENCY IN SPANISH

The Foreign Language Teacher's Handbook: Aiming for Proficiency in Spanish is a novice level instruction and assessment guide written independently by teachers for their colleagues.

Since 1989, our growing team of world language teachers has dedicated itself to creating practical, easy-to-use communicative materials for the proficiency-driven classroom. Our aim is foreign language proficiency for every student in the class.

Each topically oriented chapter of *The Foreign Language Teacher's Handbook: Aiming for Proficiency in Spanish* includes a teacher's reference of core vocabulary, pre-testing activities and a proficiency-geared chapter test. Additionally, there is also a culminating final examination. In our newly revised and expanded edition, for each chapter, there are new, more demanding writing tasks, topical authentic/portfolio assessment projects, school-to-work strategies, and useful cultural concepts including proverbs. For the teacher's information, there is a section on the euro.

The Foreign Language Teacher's Handbook series may be used to enhance a pre-existing program of instruction, or in conjunction with student texts: *C'est Ton Tour* (French), *Du Bist Dran* (German), *Toca a Te* (Italian) and *Te Toca a Ti* (Spanish).

Consistent with the National Standards, *The Foreign Language Teacher's Handbook: Aiming for Proficiency in Spanish* facilitates teaching by providing a more efficient focus on what is really needed for successful student foreign language proficiency.

ACKNOWLEDGMENTS

We are grateful to the following people for their assistance in the creation and publication of this book:

For their guidance: Walter Kleinmann, John McMorrow, Howard White, and David Kreutz

For their technical assistance: Odile Benot, Kathleen Haudberg, Patricia O'Leary, John Christianson, Vincent DiMartino, Howard Moore, Kim Catanzano, Tara Catanzano, Lucille Gruberg, Thomas Nugent and Jennifer Gordon-Tennant

For artwork: Lisa Huckstadt and Doug Moore

For their understanding and support, we give special thanks to our families.

TABLE OF CONTENTS

Authentic Assessment

AUTHENTIC ASSESSMENT

Authentic assessment, or performance based assessment, attempts to evaluate students by processes similar to those used to gauge accomplishment in the world beyond the classroom. It involves a more extensive process of judgment by the teacher and a multiplicity of products on which the students are to be evaluated.

Performance based assessment can include recorded conversations in a foreign language, laboratory experiments, individual and group projects, responses to open ended questions, exhibitions, interviews and portfolios. Students are expected to perform intellectual tasks such as face to face conversations, translations, analyses, speculations, and explanations.

Rubrics or assessment measurement guides must be given to students so they may understand how they must perform in order to achieve maximum results.

Authentic assessment is used by the foreign language teacher to evaluate the progress of students in the four skills in the language being studied. The best examples of this type of assessment are kept in portfolios beginning with the first level of language studied.

Portfolios assess the progress of students over the course of several years through papers, audio tapes, video tapes, written work , etc. selected by the students and the teacher. The selected work provides evidence of student self-reflection and it allows the student to see his or her progress. Portfolios can be kept on compact discs, if facilities are available. Computer programs on CD-Rom allow for interactive participation for the student. Computers with CD-Rom capabilities can be used in place of a language laboratory to record auditory tapes. Portfolios monitor the students' growth over time and heighten their awareness of the process of language learning. They show thought and process and highlight the students' best work. Portfolios reflect real, authentic, learning activities. Students may even include their own comments about their progress and goals.

Portfolios are used to place students correctly in their appropriate level of foreign language study. They can be used as a device for communication with subsequent teachers as well as a basis for communication with parents. They can provide a sense of personal history for the student. Portfolios can also be used to demonstrate the effectiveness of a school curriculum.

AUTHENTIC ASSESSMENT

Assessment Projects are provided for each topic. They are designed to be authentic and meaningful. Multi-disciplinary assessment tasks and projects can effectively simulate real-life contexts a student could encounter. Assessment tasks should make students demonstrate critical thinking, problem solving and collaboration skills. The standards of excellence (RUBRICS) should be clearly outlined to students before they begin the assessment task. Keep in mind that the point system must be changed according to the points allotted for each item in the project. This is at the teacher's discretion. There are also additional assessment tools that can be used in conjunction with the tests and projects or as individual assessment instruments. They are located with the projects.

Rubrics clearly state what a student can do. Samples of rubrics for speaking and composition writing for a novice level student are given in this chapter. They may be followed as presented or modified by the individual teacher. The number of points allowed may be changed according to the project or situation being evaluated.

An *Oral Evaluation Score Sheet* has been developed to help teachers score speaking tasks quickly and efficiently. By cutting the sheet in half, the teacher will have a record of each speaking grade for every student, if four students are evaluated per sheet. Using the grid on the left, the teacher makes a record of the student's speaking performance grade. The student's duplicate record on the right may be attached to his/her test paper. In this way the student will know which aspect of speaking needs to be improved.

EVALUATION RUBRICS FOR THE BEGINNING LEVEL

ORAL

PRONUNCIATION

5
Generally phonetically correct and very comprehensible; with minor errors

3
Errors in pronunciation; guesses at words; no interference with communication

1
Many errors which interfere with communication

0
Incomprehensible and inappropriate

FLUENCY

5
Smooth delivery; some self-correcting; hesitates but communicates easily

3
Occasional halting and fragmentary delivery; is able to rephrase

1
Frequent halting; repeats the question word before responses

0
Incomprehensible and inappropriate

VOCABULARY

5
Very good vocabulary use; words are appropriate

3
Vocabulary is adequate; limited use of basic words

1
Inadequate vocabulary or incorrect use of words

0
Incomprehensible and inappropriate

SYNTAX

5
Minor errors in structure which do not interfere with communication

3
Occasional grammatical errors; some are self-corrected

1
Many errors in agreement or verb forms; errors in basic grammar.

0
Incomprehensible and inappropriate

5

SCORE SHEET FOR ORAL EVALUATION

NAME _____

Pronunciation	5	3	1	0
Fluency	5	3	1	0
Vocabulary	5	3	1	0
Syntax	5	3	1	0

Total _____ /20

NAME _____

Pronunciation	5	3	1	0
Fluency	5	3	1	0
Vocabulary	5	3	1	0
Syntax	5	3	1	0

Total _____ /20

NAME _____

Pronunciation	5	3	1	0
Fluency	5	3	1	0
Vocabulary	5	3	1	0
Syntax	5	3	1	0

Total _____ /20

NAME _____

Pronunciation	5	3	1	0
Fluency	5	3	1	0
Vocabulary	5	3	1	0
Syntax	5	3	1	0

Total _____ /20

NAME _____

Pronunciation	5	3	1	0
Fluency	5	3	1	0
Vocabulary	5	3	1	0
Syntax	5	3	1	0

Total _____ /20

NAME _____

Pronunciation	5	3	1	0
Fluency	5	3	1	0
Vocabulary	5	3	1	0
Syntax	5	3	1	0

Total _____ /20

NAME _____

Pronunciation	5	3	1	0
Fluency	5	3	1	0
Vocabulary	5	3	1	0
Syntax	5	3	1	0

Total _____ /20

NAME _____

Pronunciation	5	3	1	0
Fluency	5	3	1	0
Vocabulary	5	3	1	0
Syntax	5	3	1	0

Total _____ /20

Student Name _____

Conversion Chart
14 - 16	= 10
11 - 13	= 8
8 - 10	= 6
5 - 7	= 4
2 - 4	= 2
0 - 1	= 0

Total Raw Score _____
Total Score _____

WRITING TASK RUBRIC

	4	3	2	1
Objective/ Task	Fulfills the task, uses appropriate ideas and presents ideas in a logical sequence.	Fulfills the task by using mostly relevant ideas.	Fulfills the task but there are some irrelevancies.	Makes at least one statement, which fulfills the task.
Vocabulary	Uses a full range of level appropriate nouns, verbs and adjectives. Uses relevant words to expand the topic.	Uses a variety of relevant and appropriate vocabulary to address the task.	Uses vocabulary that is sometimes not appropriate or relevant to the task.	Uses limited vocabulary, which is often inappropriate for the task.
Structure	Demonstrates a high degree of control of structure: • Subject/verb agreement • Noun/adjective agreement • Correct word order • Spelling Errors **do not** impede the overall comprehensibility of the passage.	Demonstrates some control of structure. • Subject/verb agreement • Noun/adjective agreement • Correct word order • Spelling Errors **do not** impede the overall comprehensibility of the passage.	Demonstrates inaccuracies in the control of structure. • Subject/verb agreement • Noun/adjective agreement • Correct word order • Spelling Errors **do** impede the overall comprehensibility of the passage.	Exhibits little control of structure. Errors hinder overall comprehensibility of passage.
Word Count * Names of people and English products do not count. (K-Mart, Pepsi)	Utilizes 30 or more comprehensible words that develop the task. (20+)	Utilizes 25 -29 comprehensible words in the target language that develop the task. (15-19)	Utilizes 20 - 24 comprehensible words in the target language that develop the task. (10-14)	Utilizes 15 - 19 comprehensible words in the target language that develop the task. (5-9)

For compositions of 20 words, use the word count in parenthesis.

- 6 -

Student Name _____Date _____

Writing Tasks Checklist

Refer to the Writing Rubrics for an explanation of each category.

	4	3	2	1	0
Objective • Satisfies the task's objective • Uses appropriate ideas • Presents ideas in a logical sequence					
Vocabulary • Uses level appropriate nouns, verbs and adjectives • Uses a variety of relevant words					
Structure • Subject/verb agreement • Noun/adjective agreement • Correct word order • Spelling					
Word Count • Comprehensible • In target language • Appropriate for the task	30+ (20+)	25-29 (15-19)	20-24 (10-14)	15-19 (5-9)	<15 (<5)

For compositions of 20 words use the word count in parenthesis.

Total Raw Score

Final Task Score

Conversion Chart

14 - 16 = 10
11 - 13 = 8
 8 - 10 = 6
 5 - 7 = 4
 2 - 4 = 2
 0 - 1 = 0

School-to-Career

SCHOOL-TO-WORK

School-to-Work (also known as School-to-Career) is a national and state initiative whose goal is to provide students with necessary tools for success in the workplace.

School-to-Work places new emphasis on relating learning to career transferable interest and skills, thus creating greater career options and professional effectiveness for more students.

Since *The New Teacher's Handbook* is geared to the novice level of language study, the book's School-to-Work activities consist of role-playing, brainstorming, research, field trips, discussions and speakers, leading to a greater awareness of foreign language as a career asset. For more advanced levels of study, internships, exchanges and volunteer work are also recommended.

This chapter includes School-to-Work information from the United States Departments of Education and Labor, plus a rationale for foreign language's inclusion in this program. The last part is a fact sheet that pinpoints the value of French studies in such a program.

SCHOOL-TO-WORK OPPORTUNITIES
U.S. DEPARTMENT OF EDUCATION   U.S. DEPARTMENT OF LABOR

SCHOOL-TO-WORK LEARNING CENTER FACT SHEET

The National School-to-Work Learning and Information Center provides information, assistance and training to build school-to-work opportunities in the United States. The Center utilizes the latest information technology to help increase the capacity of professionals, and to develop and implement School-to-Work systems across the nation. Its services are available to state and local School-to-Work offices, employers, schools, labor, parents, students, and to the general public.

The Center functions as the national hub for synthesizing, communicating, and disseminating information that is essential to creating School-to-Work opportunities across the country. Operating under the School-to-Work Opportunities Act, the Center serves as a broker of technical assistance expertise in the fields of School-to-Work system building, school-based learning, work-based learning, and connecting activities.

SCHOOL-TO-WORK OPPORTUNITIES

The Center will serve as a national repository of information on:

- Successful school-to-work systems, professional development strategies, management of state and local partnerships, integrated curricula, career awareness, and methods for involving employers.

- Labor market analyses, surveys, and other information related to the economic environment

- Research and evaluation concerning school-to-work, skill certificates, skill standards, and related assessment technologies.

Guided by experts in the field, the Center offers customers access through six distinct services:

- A resource bank of select technical assistance providers
- An 800-number "Answer Line"
- An Internet Home Page/Information Network (http://www.stw.ed.gov)
- Databases on key School-to-Work contacts, organizations, and practices
- Relevant publications
- Meetings, conferences, and training sessions

The Center is dedicated to total customer satisfaction. Operated by DTI and the Academy for Educational Development, the Center is open from 8:00 a.m. to 6:00 p.m. (ET). For further information about the National School-to-Work Learning and Information Center, please contact:

NATIONAL SCHOOL-TO-WORK LEARNING AND INFORMATION CENTER
400 Virginia Avenue, SW
Room 210
Washington, DC 20024

Tel. (800) 251-7236
Fax: (202) 401-6211
E-mail: stw-ic@ed.gov
Internet: http://www.stw.ed.gov

FOREIGN LANGUAGES AND BUSINESS

"The international language of business is English!" Is this comment valid or is it time to ensure the next generation of American business people and students make the effort to learn the languages of the world? Knowing the language and culture of the customer can make the difference between success or failure around the globe.

Personal Relationships

The ability to develop a personal relationship with a customer is crucial in creating a rapport to foster long-term trust, loyalty and business. The business person who can speak the language of the customer and understand his/her culture has a definite advantage in all the social relations that are expected in the business world, which can include networking with the customer and attending social gatherings.

Even when business people from other countries know English, they are honored that Americans make the effort to speak their language. Frequently, in other countries, company executives want to get to know you first before doing business. It's a matter of gaining trust.

Customer Comfort

It is good business practice to make a customer feel comfortable. Some business people who have studied English as a foreign language may not feel totally comfortable using English. When they are involved in complicated business transactions, it is a definite asset for the American to have a knowledge of the foreign business person's language.

Competition for the Customer

The point of developing a good personal relationship with a foreign customer and showing respect for his or her culture, is to develop trust and loyalty so he or she will prefer to do business with you. Where there are competitors, knowing the customer's language is crucial. Moreover, American firms which lack individuals who can communicate in other languages, can only do business with foreign companies who have English-speaking personnel.

Advantages in Negotiations

During negotiations, American business people should have strong interests in being able to understand what foreign negotiators are discussing in their own language. In order for American business people to be on an equal footing, competency in the language of the foreign negotiating team is essential.

FOREIGN LANGUAGES AND BUSINESS

Functioning Globally

World trade often requires business people to live in or travel to different countries. It is a great advantage to know the language of the country one is living in or visiting. When living in or traveling to another country, it is helpful to be able to speak to the local people in their language. This gives a view from another perspective of a particular country and facilitates one's stay.

Studying a language further increases tolerance of non-English-speaking people, thereby teaching one to be courteous to others.

In the hotel industry, it is very desirable for employees to know the language of the tourist. Convention and visitor bureaus often keep lists of languages and hotels that provide services in those languages.

As companies realize the Internet is a viable way to sell their products, translation firms report they are increasingly requested to translate Internet services into other languages.

Multilingual American business people have the advantage of speaking to local distributors in other countries on a personal basis, and can attend to the specific needs of these customers. Often product labels and directions destined for export must be translated into more than one language. For example, American products for sale in Quebec must be written in French. American companies do not have the option of solely writing labels and directions in English.

Conclusion

Business people who can communicate effectively in at least one foreign language and have a sensitivity to cultural differences, are major assets to companies succeeding internationally. Business people who have successfully learned one language are better able to acquire additional languages. If we invest the time and effort to learn the languages of our trading partners, we will gain a competitive edge and will possess the cultural insight to function more fully in the twenty-first century.

Foreign Languages and Business is adapted from an article by Dr. Louise Terry and Judy Martialay, Co-chairs of the Legislative Committee, New York State Association of Foreign Language Teachers

The Euro

THE EURO

On January 1, 1999, the euro was born in Europe, creating one market, one central bank, one currency. Not since the time of the Roman Empire has there been one common European currency. As a result of this birth, the 12 participating countries of the European Union essentially have the same inflation targets, interest rates and economic policy goals. Trade should also increase within Europe since foreign exchange rates have now been eliminated.

The euro created fixed conversion rates (The French franc was fixed on January 1, 1999, at 6.65 to one euro.) among the participating countries. Banks, stock exchanges and all citizens now do business in euros. Monetary policy is regulated by the new European Central Bank located in Frankfurt am Main, Germany.

On January 1, 2002, euro bills and coins went into circulation, and on March 1, 2002, all national bills and coins ceased to be legal tender. All European currencies as we knew them do not exist; the French franc is only a memory.

Austria, Belgium, Finland, France (including the overseas departments of Réunion, Guadeloupe, Martinique and Guyana, as well as St-Pierre-et-Miquelon and Mayotte), Germany, Greece, Ireland, Italy, Luxembourg, Netherlands, Portugal and Spain are the participating members of the euro, having met the criteria established by the European Union (budget debt should be no more than 3% of the gross domestic product, inflation should be no more than 3% , and the overall government debt should be less than 60% of the gross domestic product). Britain, Denmark and Sweden have decided to delay their entry into using the euro. (Thus, there are 15 member states of the European Union, 12 participating in the euro.) Norway and Switzerland are not members of the European Union and will therefore not be using the euro as a national currency.

The euro coins are as follows: 1 cent, 2 cents and 5 cents which are copper colored; 10 cents, 20 cents and 50 cents which are brass colored; 1 euro is silver colored with an outer brass colored ring and the two euros coin is brass colored with an outer silver ring. The bill denominations are: 5 (grayish), 10 (reddish), 20 (bluish), 50 (orange), 100 (greenish) , 200 (yellowish) and 500 (pale violet) euros. Each coin has a European side (the same in all countries and carry the value of the coin) and a national side on which each country has its own design. The French coins carry the letters RF (République Française). The designs of the bills are architecturally generic – windows, gateways and bridges that depict 7 periods of European architectural cultural history: Classical, Romanesque, Gothic, Renaissance, Baroque and Rococo, the age of iron and glass architecture, modern 21st century architecture – and do not reflect any particular culture or

THE EURO

country. A map of Europe showing the European Union also appears on the bills. Three years were required to mint all the necessary coinage, 2.5 million bills and 7 million coins every day, for a total of 2.5 billion bills and 6.6 billion coins.

The symbol for the euro (€) is similar to epsilon, the Greek parent of the Roman letter-e, and a tribute to Greece as the cradle of European civilization. The parallel lines symbolize stability, and their ends are slanted to make its from more dynamic. The European Union's Monetary Commission states this symbol is to transcend all languages within the euro zone, or euro land (also spelled Euroland). In Spanish the word is written in lower case letters.

Therefore, to calculate the number of euros equal to a certain number of pesetas you must divide the number of pesetas by 166.386 and round off to the nearest decimal. For example, 1,000 pts. equals 6.01€. A movie ticket for 700 pts. is worth 4.21€. A newspaper for 350 pts. is worth .51€. Jeans for 6,000 pts. are worth 36.06€.

To obtain current euro rates, consult the Proficiency Press Web site: http://www.proficiencypress.com.

PERSONAL
IDENTIFICATION

La Información Biográfica:

señor	la nacionalidad
señora	norteamericano,a
señorita	los Estados Unidos
el nombre	puertorriqueño,a
el apellido	latinoamericano,a
la dirección	español
el pueblo	inglés, inglesa
la ciudad	italiano,a
el estado	alemán, alemana
el código postal	la profesión
el país	el alumno
el número de teléfono	la alumna
el domicilio	el profesor
la fecha	la profesora
el nacimiento	

La Familia

el padre	la madre
el hermano	la hermana
el esposo	la esposa
el hombre	la mujer
el muchacho	la muchacha
el amigo	la amiga
mi/mis	el niño,
su/sus, tu,tus	la niña

Las Características Físicas

alto,a	bajo,a
grande	pequeño,a
gordo,a	flaco,a
bonito,a	guapo,a
joven	viejo,a
rubio,a	moreno,a
pelirrojo,a	delgado,a
fuerte	débil
los ojos: azules, de color café, castaños, pardos, verdes, negros	el pelo: rubio, moreno, gris, negro, castaño, largo, corto
bueno,a	malo,a
estúpido,a	inteligente
tonto,a	simpático,a
bien	mal
antipático,a	generoso,a
paciente	feliz

Las Expresiones:

¿Cómo se llama Ud.?   Me llamo....
¿Cómo te llamas?

¿Cuál es su (tu) nombre?   Mi nombre es....
¿Cuántos años tiene Ud.?   Tengo.....años.
¿Cuántos años tienes?

¿De dónde es Ud.?   Soy de...

¿De dónde eres?
¿Cuál es su (tu) nacionalidad?   Soy....

¿Cuándo es su (tu) cumpleaños?   ¿Cuál es su (tu) número de teléfono?
¿Cuál es su (tu) fecha de nacimiento? ¿Cuál es su (tu) dirección?

¿Cuál es su (tu) lugar de nacimiento? ¿Cuándo nació Ud.?

¿Dónde naciste?   ¿Cuándo naciste?
¿Dónde nació Ud.?
¿Dónde vive Ud.?   Vivo en....
¿Dónde vives?
¿Cuántos hermanos tiene Ud.?   Tengo....

¿Cuántos hermanos tienes?

PERSONAL IDENTIFICATION

¿Cómo es Ud.?   Soy....

¿Cómo eres?
¿Cómo está Ud.?   Estoy _____.

¿Cómo estás?
¿Qué tal?

¿De qué color es el pelo de _____?   ¿De qué color son los ojos de _____?
¿Qué le (te) gusta (hacer)?   Me gusta_____.
                                                No me gusta _____.

                                                Prefiero _____.

                                                Odio _____.
sí   perdón
no   por favor
un poco   gracias

Las Actividades:

llamar   vivir
nacer   hablar
bailar   mirar la televisión
leer   trabajar
comer   cocinar
dormir   hacer la tarea
viajar   estudiar
escuchar la música   cantar

lavar los platos   nadar
esquiar   salir con amigos
gustar   preferir
odiar   jugar (a los deportes, al béisbol, al fútbol
                                                americano, al tenis, al fútbol, al voléibol)

Los Días de la Semana   ## Los Meses del Año

lunes   enero
martes   febrero   agosto
miércoles   marzo   septiembre
jueves   abril   octubre
viernes   mayo   noviembre
sábado   junio   diciembre
domingo   julio

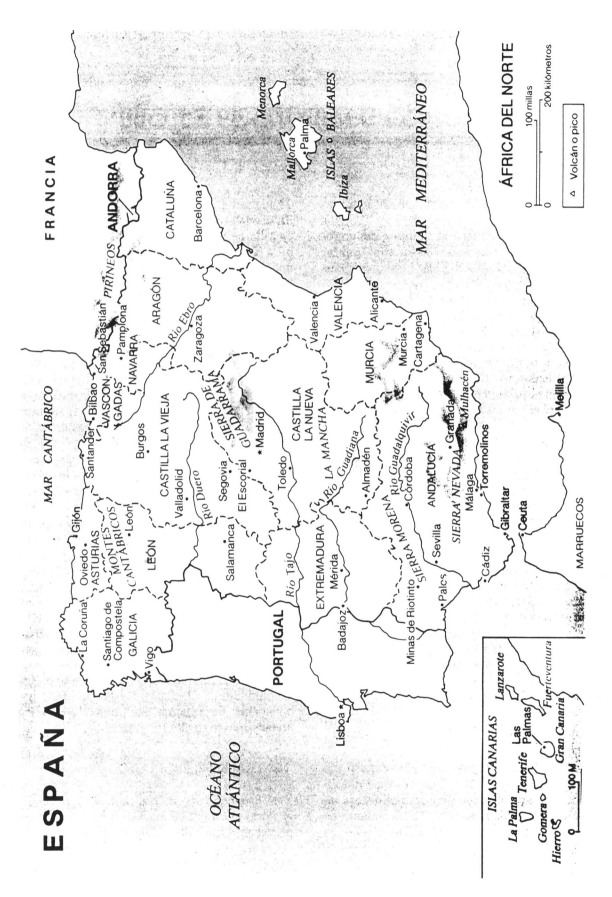

ESPAÑA

FRANCIA

OCÉANO ATLÁNTICO

MAR CANTÁBRICO

MAR MEDITERRÁNEO

ÁFRICA DEL NORTE

PIRINEOS
ANDORRA
CATALUÑA
Barcelona

ARAGÓN
NAVARRA
Pamplona
Zaragoza
Río Ebro

VASCON-
GADAS
San Sebastián
Bilbao
Santander

Gijón
Oviedo
ASTURIAS
MONTES CANTÁBRICOS
León
CASTILLA LA VIEJA
Burgos
Valladolid
Río Duero

La Coruña
Santiago de Compostela
GALICIA
Vigo

LEÓN
Salamanca

SIERRA DE GUADARRAMA
Segovia
El Escorial
Madrid
Toledo

CASTILLA LA NUEVA
LA MANCHA

VALENCIA
Valencia
Alicante

MURCIA
Murcia
Cartagena

Río Guadiana
Almadén

Río Guadalquivir
Córdoba
SIERRA MORENA

ANDALUCÍA
SIERRA NEVADA
Granada
Mulhacén
Málaga
Torremolinos

Sevilla
Cádiz
Palos
Minas de Riotinto

Gibraltar
Ceuta
Melilla

MARRUECOS

EXTREMADURA
Mérida
Badajoz
Río Tajo

PORTUGAL
Lisboa

ISLAS BALEARES
Menorca
Mallorca
Palma
Ibiza

ISLAS CANARIAS
La Palma
Tenerife
Gomera
Hierro
Las Palmas
Gran Canaria
Lanzarote
Fuerteventura
100 M

100 millas
200 kilómetros
△ Volcán o pico

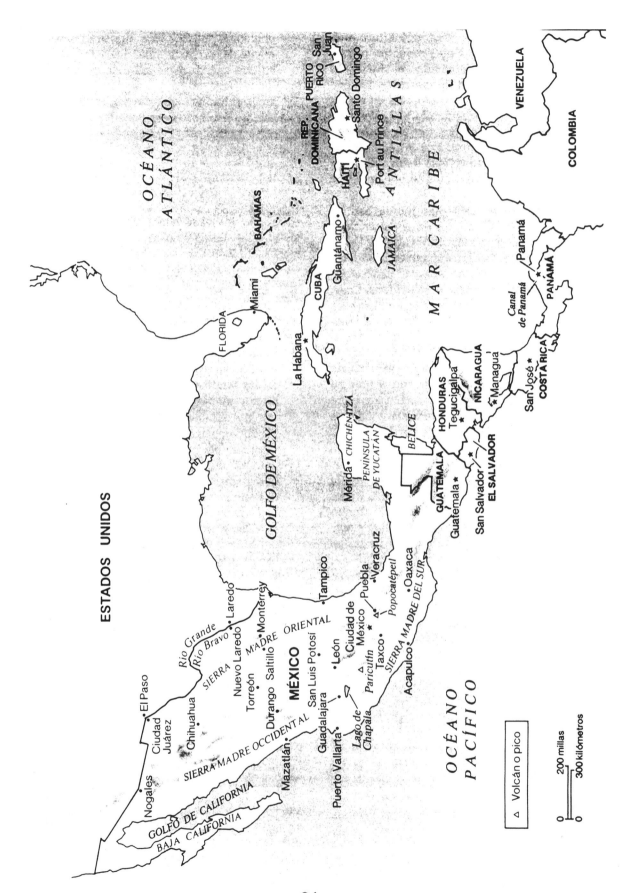

MAR CARIBE

OCÉANO ATLÁNTICO

Barranquilla
Cartagena

La Guaira
Caracas

Medellín

Río Orinoco

LLANOS

VENEZUELA

GUYANA

SURINAM

GUAYANA
FRANCESA

*Bogotá

Río Magdalena

COLOMBIA

Quito *
Cotopaxi
Chimborazo

Ecuador

Guayaquil

ECUADOR

Río Amazonas

LOS ANDES

PERÚ
Callao

Cuzco

Lima

BRASIL

*Lago
Titicaca*

*La Paz

BOLIVIA

*Brasilia

OCÉANO
PACÍFICO

LOS ANDES

*Desierto de
Atacama*

GRAN CHACO

Río Paraguay

PARAGUAY
Asunción*

Tucumán

Río de Janeiro

Iguazú

CHILE

Córdoba

Río Paraná

URUGUAY

Aconcagua

Rosario

Viña del Mar
Valparaíso

Buenos Aires

Montevideo

Santiago

Río de la Plata

OCÉANO
ATLÁNTICO

*Islas Juan
Fernández
(Ch.)*

PAMPAS

ARGENTINA

PATAGONIA

*Estrecho
De
Magallanes*

*Islas Malvinas
(Falkland Islands)
(Ing.)*

Tierra del Fuego

*Cabo de
Hornos*

0   300 millas

0   500 kilómetros

△   Volcán o pico

- 25 -

PERSONAL IDENTIFICATION

PRE-TESTING ACTIVITIES

1. Students make their own identification cards. Teacher takes a photograph of the students in groups of 6. When the photos are developed, the teacher cuts them into six individual pictures. The students can prepare an index card with their vital information in Spanish (leaving a place for the photo). Then the students affix the photo to the card and laminate it with clear contact paper.

2. Students complete biographical order forms from ads, subscriptions, etc.

3. Teacher records on tape native speakers giving biographical information. Students complete forms from what they hear on the tape.

4. Students interview each other. Each completes a biographical form for the other student interviewed. Setting: Passport Office.

5. Students choose a person from a magazine and give this person an identity. Students verbally describe this person biographically, physically and psychologically. Then they write down this information in paragraph form.

6. Students can read pen pal ads from a Spanish magazine. Afterwards they can write an ad themselves (excluding their names). Teacher can compile the ads, photocopy them and distribute them to the class. The students can try to guess who wrote them.

7. The alphabet can be practiced by playing Hangman, or BRAVO, a form of the game, Bingo.

USEFUL CULTURAL CONCEPTS FOR THIS CHAPTER

- The European greeting - kissing on both cheeks when meeting
- Waving - the opposite direction
- Writing the date (day, month, year)
- Writing street addresses (number last)
- "*Quinceañera*" - 15th birthday of Hispanic girls
- The importance of godparents and their roll in the "*quinceañera*"
- Maps: Latin American countries, capitals and their locations.
- Celebrating one's saint's day as well as one's birthday

Los Refranes:

- Más vale estar sólo que mal acompañado.
- Los niños y los locos dicen las verdades.
- Dime con quien andas y te diré quien eres.

PERSONAL IDENTIFICATION

SCHOOL - TO - WORK

Referring to the map, Los Países Hispanos, brainstorm with students how Spanish could be a useful language to know.

SPEAKING SITUATIONS FOR PART I OF THE EXAM (30%)

1. You are on vacation in Mexico. Upon arrival, the customs official asks you a few questions.

2. You are at a Spanish fiesta and are dancing with your friend's cousin. Socialize with this person. Find out his/her name and interests.

3. You have been chosen to interview the new student from El Salvador so that you can introduce him/her to the class.

TEACHER'S SCRIPT FOR THE EXAM, PART II (Listening, 30%)

Part 2a Directions: For each question, you will hear some background information in English. Then you will hear a passage in Spanish twice, followed by a question in English. Listen carefully. After you have heard the question, read the question and the four suggested answers. Choose the best answer and write its number in the appropriate space on your answer sheet. (9%)

1.   Your Spanish pen pal is visiting you. He says:

Me gusta leer. Me encantan los libros. Odio los deportes y no me gustan ni las películas ni los programas de televisión.

Based on what your pen pal has said, how will you spend the afternoon with him? (3)

2.   You are talking to your friend about his girlfriend Ana. He says:

Ana es muy simpática e inteligente. Ella tiene los ojos de color café y es rubia.

What statement is true about Ana? (4)

PERSONAL IDENTIFICATION

3.   You are walking in town in Spain with your mother and you encounter a little girl who is lost. Your mother talks to the lost child. She says:

   - ¿Cómo te llamas?
   - Luisa
   - ¿Cuál es tu apellido?
   - Sánchez.
   - ¿Dónde vives?
   - en la calle Rivera, número 13

   On what street does the little girl live? (1)

Part 2B Directions: For each question, you will hear some background information in English. Then you will hear a passage in Spanish twice, followed by a question in Spanish. Listen carefully. After you have heard the question, read the question and the four suggested answers. Choose the best answer and write its number in the appropriate space on your answer sheet. (9%)

4.   You are listening to your friend's Spanish grandmother, Sra. García, talk about herself.

   Mi cumpleaños es mañana. Nací el 3 de agosto de 1942 en Madrid, la capital de España. Tengo 4 hermanos. Me gusta mucho este país, pero me gusta España también.

   ¿Cuál es la fecha del nacimiento de la Sra. García? (2)

5.   Your friend is telling you about his family. He says:

   Vivo en Nueva York y hablo inglés. Hablo español también porque mi padre es puertorriqueño. Hablo italiano porque mi madre es de Italia.

   El padre de tu amigo es de..... (1)

6.   Your aunt from Mexico is telling you about her work.

   Tengo 32 alumnos en mi clase. Tengo los muchachos de 6 años de edad. Me gusta mucho mi profesión.

   ¿Cuál es su profesión? (3)

PERSONAL IDENTIFICATION

Part 2c Directions: For each question, you will hear some background information in English. Then you will hear a passage in Spanish twice, followed by a question in English. Listen carefully. After you have heard the question, read the question and look at the 4 pictures on your test. Choose the picture that best answers the question and write its number in the appropriate space on your answer sheet. (12%)

7. Your friend is showing you her family album of photos. She is speaking about her father. She says:

    Mi padre tiene el pelo rubio y es gordo. Él es muy simpático.

    Which person is your friend's father? (3)

8. Your friend is telling you what he does during the weekend. He says:

    No me gusta hacer la tarea los domingos. Prefiero jugar con mi amigo en el parque.

    What does your friend do on Sunday? (1)

9. You must pick up your friend's cousin at the train station. Your friend gives the following description of her cousin Mónica. She says:

    Mónica tiene 20 años. Ella tiene el pelo corto. También es flaca y morena.

    Which person is Mónica? (3)

10. You are helping Señora López clean up her son's room. She says:

    A mi hijo, Roberto, le gusta mucho leer. Tiene muchos libros. No le gusta escuchar la música.

    Which are Roberto's belongings? (4)

Listening Comprehension Answers:
For all chapters, the answers are indicated in parenthesis following each question. (See questions 1-10 on the previous pages.)

Reading Comprehension answers:

3a (8%)   11 __1__   12 __4__   13 __3__   14 __2__

3b (12%)   15 __1__   16 __4__   17 __1__   18 __1__

Nombre _____ Fecha _____

EXAMINATION

Part I SPEAKING (30%)
Part 2 LISTENING (30%)

Part 2a Directions: For each question, you will hear some background information in English. Then you will hear a passage in Spanish twice, followed by a question in English. Listen carefully. After you have heard the question, read the question and the four suggested answers. Choose the best answer and write its number in the appropriate space on your answer sheet (9%).

1. Based on what your pen pal has said, how will you spend the afternoon with him?
   1. playing tennis
   2. going to the movies
   3. visiting the library
   4. watching television

2. What statement is true about Ana?
   1. She is tall.
   2. She is stupid.
   3. She has black hair.
   4. She has brown eyes.

3. On what street does the little girl live?
   1. Rivera
   2. Luisa
   3. Sánchez
   4. los Estados Unidos

Part 2b Directions: For each question, you will hear some background information in English. Then you will hear a passage in Spanish twice, followed by a question in Spanish. Listen carefully. After you have heard the question, read the question and the four suggested answers. Choose the best answer and write its number in the appropriate space on your answer sheet (9%).

4. ¿Cuál es la fecha del nacimiento de la Sra. García?
   1. 4 hermanos
   2. el 3 de agosto
   3. los Estados Unidos
   4. España

5. El padre de tu amigo es de...
   1. Puerto Rico
   2. Italia
   3. los Estados Unidos
   4. España

6. ¿Cuál es su profesión?
   1. Ella es madre.
   2. Ella es alumna.
   3. Ella es profesora.
   4. Ella es artista.

PERSONAL IDENTIFICATION

Part 2c Directions: For each question, you will hear some background information in English. Then you will hear a passage in Spanish twice, followed by a question in English. Listen carefully. After you have heard the question, read the question and look at the 4 pictures on your test. Choose the picture that best answers the question and write its number in the appropriate space on your answer sheet (12%).

7. Which person is your friend's father?

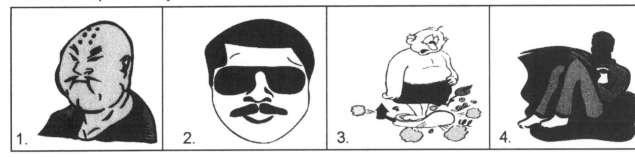

8. What does your friend do on Sunday?

9. Which person is Monica?

10. Which are Roberto's belongings?

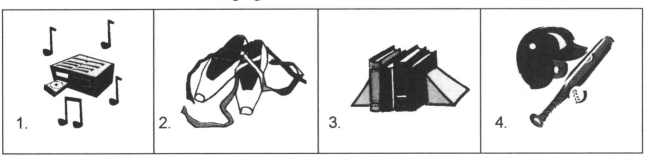

Part 3 READING (20%)

Part 3a Directions: Answer the questions in English based on the reading selections in Spanish. Choose the best answer to each question. Base your choice on the content of the reading selection. Write the number of your answer in the appropriate space on your answer sheet (8%).

Ayuntamiento de Barcelona

Nombre y Apellido: _Pilar Gómez de Fernádez_

Fecha de nacimiento: _el seis de julio de 1952_

Lugar: _Barcelona, España_

Profesión:
_____Artista_____

Domicilio: _calle Londres 9, 3ª, Sevilla_

Destino: _Estados Unidos_

Firma: __Pilar Gómez de Fernández__   Fecha: ____

---

11.   Based on this form, what statement is true about the person completing it?
   1. She was born in July.   3. She lives in Barcelona.
   2. She is going to England.   4. Her last name is Pilar.

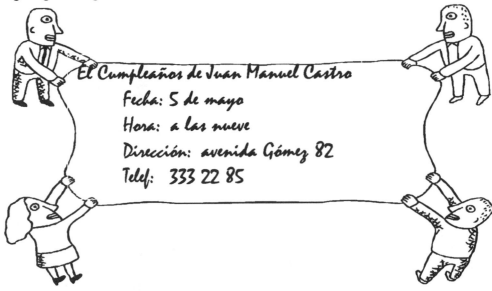

El Cumpleaños de Juan Manuel Castro
Fecha: 5 de mayo
Hora: a las nueve
Dirección: avenida Gómez 82
Teléf: 333 22 85

12.   What is this invitation for?
   1. a block party   3. a party at 5 de Mayo Avenue
   2. the marriage of Juan   4. Juan Manuel's birthday

Los Señores José Ortega y Fernández
Anuncian el nacimiento de su bebé
María Luisa
El 8 de junio
En Salamanca

13. What would you do upon receiving this card?
    1. prepare for a marriage   3. buy a baby present
    2. pack for a vacation   4. send a toy for a little boy

VACACIONES AEROLATINAS

1. Nombre y Apellido _____
2. Dirección _____
3. País de nacimiento _____
4. Nacionalidad _____
5. Destino del viaje _____
6. Fecha del viaje _____

14. Which item on this form do you fill out to tell where you live?
    1. (1)   3. (3)
    2. (2)   4. (5)

Part 3b Directions: Answer the questions in Spanish based on the reading selections in Spanish. Choose the best answer to each question. Base your choice on the content of the reading selection. Write the number of your answer in the appropriate space on your answer sheet (12%).

(1)

Español. Quiero amigos de N.Y. Me gustan Menudo, L.L. Cool J y los New Kids on the Block!!!

(3)

Mexicano. Me gustan los Mets, los Giants, y los Celtics también. ¿ A tí también? Escríbeme.

(2)

Chileno. Mi clase favorita es español. Las matemáticas son buenas también. Escribe.

(4)

Colombiano. Me gusta Stephen King, Shakespeare, y F. Scott Fitzgerald. Me encanta la literatura.

15. ¿Quién escucha la música?
    1. (1)   3. (3)
    2. (2)   4. (5)

16. ¿A quién le gusta leer?
    1. (1)   3. (3)
    2. (2)   4. (4)

El Noticiero

Gloria Estefan, cantante famosa del grupo "Miami Sound Machine", nació el primero de septiembre de 1957 en la Havana, Cuba. Ella vive en Miami con su esposo, Emilio Estefan y su hijo de 18 años, Nayeb. Ella tiene los ojos pardos y el pelo castaño. A Gloria le gusta leer y cocinar. "Conga" y "Bad Boys" son los éxitos más populares de esta cantante famosa.

17. ¿Cuántos hijos tiene Gloria Estefan?
    1. uno   3. ocho
    2. dos   4. cinco

18. Según este artículo...
    1. Gloria vive en Florida.
    2. A Gloria no le gusta leer.
    3. Gloria es rubia.
    4. Gloria tiene los ojos azules.

Part 4 WRITING (20%)

Part 4 Directions: Choose two of the three writing tasks provided below. Your answer to each of the two questions should be written entirely in Spanish and should contain a minimum of **20 words**.

Place names and brand names written in Spanish count as one word. Contractions are counted as one word. Salutations, closing, and commonly used abbreviations are included in the word count. Numbers, unless written as words, and names of people do not count as words.

Be sure that you have satisfied the purpose of the task. The sentence structure and/or expressions used should be connected logically and demonstrate a wide range of vocabulary with minimal repetition.

4a. You have just been given the name of your Spanish pen pal. Write a note in Spanish to your pen pal describing yourself. You may wish to include:

- Your name, nationality, address
- Your physical appearance, color of hair, eyes, etc.
- Your personality traits
- Your likes and dislikes

4b. Write a message in Spanish to your Spanish key-pal telling him or her about one or more of your favorite friends. You may wish to include:

- His or her name and nationality
- His or her physical appearance
- His or her preferences
- His or her pastimes

4c. Your pen pal is coming to visit you soon. You would like to know about him or her before he or she arrives. Write a note to your pen pal asking him or her personal questions. You may wish to include:

- Questions about his or her age
- A question about his or her appearance
- Questions about his or her likes and dislikes
- Questions about his or her family

ANSWER SHEET

Nombre y Apellido _____ Fecha _____

Part I   **Speaking** _____ (30%)
Part 2   **Listening (30%)**   **PART 3: READING** (20%)

    2a.   2b.   2c.   3a.(8%)   3b.(12%)

1._____   4._____   7._____   11._____   15._____

2._____   5._____   8._____   12._____   16._____

3._____   6._____   9._____   13._____   17._____

                         10._____   14._____   18._____

Part 4   **Writing (20%) 20 words   Write 2 paragraphs   4a , 4b or 4c**

1_____

_____

_____

_____

_____

_____

_____

_____

_____

_____

2_____

_____

_____

_____

_____

_____

_____

_____

_____

_____

_____

PERSONAL IDENTIFICATION

AUTHENTIC ASSESSMENT

Taking Steps to Become a Foreign Exchange Student

Situation: You have been selected to travel to Costa Rica as part of a student exchange program.

1. In order to facilitated your stay in Costa Rica, the foreign exchange association requires you to make an audio or video tape about yourself. Record in Spanish information about yourself. Tell your age, your family members, your likes and dislikes, and where you live. Explain why you want to visit Costa Rica.

2. To assist with the foreign exchange program, listen to the tapes of your classmates played by your teacher. Based on what you hear on the tapes, complete the forms below.

Nombre de estudiante: _____ Le gusta: _____ No le gusta: _____ Yo comprendo: ____ muy bien el mensaje ____ más o menos ____ mal	Nombre de estudiante: _____ Le gusta: _____ No le gusta: _____ Yo comprendo: ____ muy bien el mensaje ____ más o menos ____ mal
Nombre de estudiante: _____ Le gusta: _____ No le gusta: _____ Yo comprendo: ____ muy bien el mensaje ____ más o menos ____ mal	Nombre de estudiante: _____ Le gusta: _____ No le gusta _____ Yo comprendo: ____ muy bien el mensaje ____ más o menos ____ mal

3. a. Research information on the Internet and/or by using reference books or brochures on Costa Rica. Choose one city for your stay in Costa Rica as an exchange student.

    b. *¡Buen Viaje!* Write a note in Spanish to your host family who will be meeting you at the airport in Spain. Introduce yourself, describe yourself physically so that your host family can find you at the airport. Based on your research, tell why you are happy to visit your host family's city.

FAMILY

La Familia

Los miembros de la familia
el padre
el papá
el abuelo
el bisabuelo
el padrino
el esposo
el hijo
el hermano
el tío
el primo
el niño
el bebé

los parientes
la madre
la mamá
la abuela
la bisabuela
la esposa
la hija
la hermana
la tía
la prima
la niña

Las Celebraciones

el cumpleaños
la quinceañera
el bautizo
el día de las madres
el día de los padres
la Navidad
el aniversario

Los Títulos

señor
señora
señorita
don
doña

Las Actividades

despertarse
ducharse
lavarse
acostarse
asistir a la universidad
visitar
trabajar
poner la mesa
sacar la basura
lavar platos
levantarse
bañarse
vestirse

los números 1-100
Time expressions

Las Expresiones

¿Cómo se llama su (tu)…?
¿Qué hace su (tu)…?
¿Cuántos años tiene su (tu)…?
¿A qué hora …?
¿Cómo estás (está)?
¿Quién?
¿Para quién?

Los Adjetivos

menor
enfermo,a
único,a
mayor
pequeño,a

FAMILY LIFE

PRE-TESTING ACTIVITIES

1. Have students prepare a family tree in Spanish. For each family member on the tree, the students should include names and ages along with their relationships to the student. The students may discuss their family trees with their partners. Display the students' work in the classroom.

2. In paired groups, students describe one of their relatives. This can be done in interview form and a short paragraph can be written for a class newsletter.

3. The class can play *La Familia Misteriosa*, which is similar to *Clue*. The teacher prepares an imaginary family of five members. For each member, list four adjectives to describe that member of the family. Make sure to use each expression twice for the different characters (see example). Then assign six students to play the different roles. (One extra student is included to answer "no" to all the questions to make the game more challenging.) Distribute the character list to the remaining students so that they can deduce who the students' characters are. They can figure this out by directing yes/no questions one by one to each character. The student who can determine the identity of all the characters wins a prize.

   Example of *La Familia Misteriosa*

la madre	el padre	el hijo	la abuela	el tío
alta	bajo	fuerte	gorda	débil
débil	gordo	alto	fuerte	antipático
inteligente	tonto	atlético	tonta	atlético
generosa	generoso	inteligente	antipática	bajo

USEFUL CULTURAL CONCEPTS FOR THIS CHAPTER

- Teach common Spanish gestures.
- Explain the extended family: grandparents, aunts, uncles, etc. living in the same house.
- Teach the forms of "you", *Ud.* and *Tú. Ud.* is formal while *Tú* is familiar.
- Explain the use of the wife's sur name. The wife keeps her maiden name and adds her husband's surname.
- Explain the use of chaperons. Young men and women were not permitted to be alone on a date. They were accompanied by a chaperone.

FAMILY LIFE

Los Refranes:

A quien Dios no le dio hijos, el Diablo le dio sobrinos.
Antes de que te cases, mira lo que haces.
Los niños y los locos dicen las verdades.

SCHOOL-TO-WORK

What expressions have you learned in this chapter that would be of use to a customs or immigration official, social worker, or census taker?

SPEAKING STITUATIONS FOR PART I OF THE EXAM (30%)

1. You are sitting in the park minding your little brother. A mother with her daughter is sitting near you. The daughter starts to play with your brother. Socialize by commenting, asking questions and answering questions about the children.

2. Your cousin is spending the summer with your family. She does no work in the house and you react to this situation by speaking to your mother.

3. You are in the cafeteria talking to a Spanish-speaking student. Ask about his or her family.

4. You would like to invite your friend for a day at your country house, but he or she is very shy. Try to convince him or her to come to your house by telling him or her about your family and the things you can do together.

FAMILY LIFE

TEACHER'S SCRIPT FOR THE EXAM, PART II (Listening, 30%)

Part 2a Directions: For each question, you will hear some background information in English. Then you will hear a passage in Spanish twice, followed by the question in English. Listen carefully. After you have heard the question, read the question and the four suggested answers. Choose the best answer and write its number in the appropriate space on your answer sheet. (9%)

1. You are talking to your Spanish-speaking friend about your family. He or she says:

    Yo tengo una familia muy grande. De todos mis parientes mi favorito es el hermano de mi mamá. Se llama Paco. Es alto, atletico y muy divertido.

    Who is your friend's favorite relative? (4)

2. Paco is describing his family to you on the telephone. He says:

    En mi familia tengo 2 hermanos y 3 hermanas. Mi abuelo vive con nosotros también.

    Which statement best describes Paco's family? (1)

3. Maria is an exchange student from Mexico. She is telling you about her daily routine. She says:

    Todos los días me despierto a las seis de la mañana. Luego me ducho y voy a la escuela. Por la noche miro la tele hasta las diez de la noche.

    At what time does Maria wake up every morning? (1)

Part 2b Directions: For each question, you will hear some background information in English. Then you will hear a passage in Spanish twice, followed by the question in Spanish. Listen carefully. After you have heard the question, read the question and the four suggested answers. Choose the best answer and write its number in the appropriate space on your answer sheet. (9%)

4. Pablo is talking about his parents who live back home in Puerto Rico. He says:

    Mis padres son muy simpáticos. Mi mamá es muy joven. Ella tiene treinta y siete años. Mi papá es viejo, tiene cuarenta y seis años.

    ¿Cómo son los padres de Pablo? (4)

5.   Ana is describing a photo of her family to you. She says:

Esta chica es mi hermana María. A ella le gusta estudiar mucho y hacer
la tarea. Este chico es mi hermano Luis. A él le gusta el béisbol pero no
le gusta la escuela. Aquí está mi mama, Catalina y mi papá, Diego.

¿Cómo es el hermano de Ana? (3)

6.   Jorge is telling you about his family in Spain. He says:

Mi familia es pequeña. Yo vivo en un pueblo pequeño con mi familia. Mi papá
trabaja en la ciudad. Mi mamá es profesora.

¿Qué hace la mama de Jorge? (1)

Part 2c Directions: For each question, you will hear some background information in
English. Then you will hear a passage in Spanish twice, followed by the question in
English. Listen carefully. After you have heard the question, read the question and look
at the four pictures. Choose the best answer and write its number in the appropriate
space on your answer sheet. (12%)

7.   While waiting at Barajas Airport in Madrid, you call your friend, José, to
find out who will come to pick you up. He says:

Mi papá es alto y flaco. También tiene el pelo castaño. El está en el
aeropuerto ahora.

Which is your friend's father? (4)

8.   Luisa is telling you about how her family shares the household activities.
She says:

A mí me gusta lavar platos, a mi hermana mayor le gusta cocinar, a mi
hermana menor le gusta sacar la basura, a mi mamá le gusta poner la
mesa, y a mi papá no le gusta hacer nada.

What does Luisa do to help? (3)

- 44 -

9. The new exchange student from Peru is telling you about her mother. She says:

    Mi mamá trabaja en la ciudad. A ella le gusta mirar programas de televisión mucho. Ella mira la tele hasta las once de la noche.

    What does her mother do after work? (3)

10. You and Enrique, your Spanish-speaking friend, are showing each other photographs of your family. Enrique says:

    Esta es una foto de mi familia. Mi familia es grande. Aquí estoy con mis hermanos. Tengo 3 hermanos y 3 hermanas.

    Which is the photo of Enrique's family? (1)

Reading Comprehension Answers:

3 a. (8%)	11. 2	12. 3	13. 1	14. 3
3 b. (12%)	15. 1	16. 3	17. 1	18. 3

FAMILY LIFE

Nombre _____ la fecha _____

EXAMINATION

PART 1   SPEAKING (30%)
PART 2   LISTENING (30%)

Part 2a Directions: For each question, you will hear some background information in English. Then you will hear a passage in Spanish twice, followed by the question in English. Listen carefully. After you have heard the question, read the question and the four suggested answers. Choose the best answer and write its number in the appropriate space on your answer sheet. (9%)

1. Who is your friend's favorite relative?
    1. his aunt   3. his brother
    2. his mother   4. his uncle

2. Which statement best describes Paco's family?
    1. He has five brothers and sisters.   3. He doesn' t have parents.
    2. His grandmother lives with him.   4. He is an only child.

3. At what time does Maria wake up every morning?
    1. at 6   3. at 7
    2. at 10   4. at 2

Part 2b Directions: For each question, you will hear some background information in English. Then you will hear a passage in Spanish twice, followed by the question in Spanish. Listen carefully. After you have heard the question, read the question and the four suggested answers. Choose the best answer and write its number in the appropriate space on your answer sheet. (9%)

4. ¿Cómo son los padres de Pablo?
    1. La madre es mayor que su esposo.
    2. Los padres tienen cuarenta años.
    3. El padre es menor que su esposa.
    4. La madre es menor que su esposo.

5. ¿Cómo es el hermano de Ana?
    1. Es inteligente.   3. Es atlético.
    2. Es guapo.   4. Es alto.

6. ¿Qué hace la mamá de Jorge?
    1. Trabaja en una escuela.   3. Estudia en la escuela.
    2. Es estudiante.   4. Vive en la ciudad.

FAMILY LIFE

Part 2c Directions: For each question, you will hear some background information in English. Then you will hear a passage in Spanish twice, followed by a question in English. Listen carefully. After you have heard the question, read the question and look at the 4 pictures on your test. Choose the picture that best answers the question and write its number in the appropriate space on your answer sheet. (12%)

7. Which is your friend's father?

8. What does Luisa do to help?

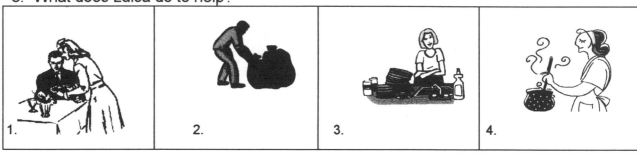

9. What does her mother do after work?

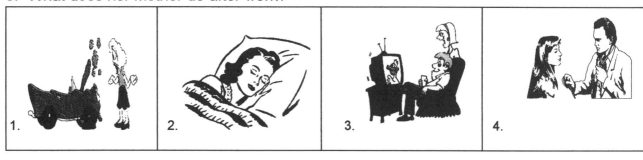

10. Which is the photo of Enrique's family?

PART 3 READING (20%)

Part 3a Directions: Answer the English questions based on a reading selections in Spanish. Choose the best answer to each question. Base your choice on the content of the reading selection. Write the number of your answer in the appropriate space on your answer sheet. (8%)

  # UNA QUINCEAÑERA

Los tíos de Alicia le invitan a Ud. para celebrar

¿Quién? *Alicia María*

¿Dónde? *Calle Primera 26*

¿Cuándo? *el 25 de junio*

**********HASTA LUEGO **********

11. For what kind of party is this invitation?
    1. Christmas
    2. a birthday
    3. a family reunion
    4. graduation

12. Who is giving the party?
    1. Alicia
    2. the parents
    3. the aunt and uncle
    4. the cousins

 ## EL NUEVO "FA"

- para lavarse en el baño
- para ducharse todos los días
- para los niños
- para los adultos

DISPONIBLE EN TU SUPERMERCADO FAVORITO

13. What product is this advertising?
    1. soap
    2. a calendar
    3. vitamins
    4. a radio

Answer this question based on the ad on the previous page.

14. This product is for...
    1. girls   3. everyone
    2. adults only   4. children only

Part 3b Directions: Answer the Spanish questions based on a reading selection in Spanish. Choose the best answer to each question. Base your choice on the content of the reading selections. Write the number of your answer in the appropriate space on your answer sheet. (12%)

DOCUMENTO DE INMIGRACIÓN

Nombre _Hector Rodríguez_
Dirección _Plaza Mayor 5_
Ciudad _Granada_ Provincia _Andalucía_
País _España_ Número del Vuelo _957_

Yo estoy con...
Esposo,a _Margarita_
Hijos _Raúl, Claudia_
Otros miembros de la familia _el tío Manuel_
Destino _Chicago_
¿Por qué? _√_ Vacaciones _____ Negocios

---

15. ¿Cuántas personas hay en esta familia?
    1. cinco   3. cuatro
    2. seis   4. tres

16. ¿Cómo se llama el hermano de Claudia?
    1. Héctor   3. Raúl
    2. Margarita   4. Manuel

    La Señora Elena Cruz nació en El Paso, Texas, el 30 de septiembre. Ella tiene cien años este año. La semana pasada la familia celebró su cumpleaños centenario en el Restaurante Flamingo.
    Su secreto por una vida tan larga es que ella duerme por diez horas cada noche y ella se despierta a las cinco de la mañana todos los días.
    En el restaurante la señora Cruz cenó con sus hijas, Lupe Cruz y Jacinta López, su hijo, Arturo y sus hermanas, María Santos y Julia Cortez, y muchos otros parientes y amigos.

17. La Señora Cruz
    1. celebró su cumpleaños en casa. 3. Tiene ochenta años.
    2. Se acuesta a medianoche.   4. Se levanta a las cinco de la mañana.

18. ¿Cuántos hijos tiene la Señora Cruz?
    1. Tiene un hijo único   3. Tiene tres hijos.
    2. Tiene muchos hijos.   4. Tiene cuatro hijos.

PART 4 WRITING (20%)
Part 4a Directions: Choose two of the three writing tasks provided below. Your answer to each of the two questions should be written entirely in Spanish and should contain a minimum of **20 words**.

    Place names and brand names written in Spanish count as one word. Contractions are counted as one word. Salutations, closing, and commonly used abbreviations are included in the word count. Numbers, unless written as words, and names of people do not count as words.

Be sure that you have satisfied the purpose of the task. The sentence structure and/or expressions used should be connected logically and demonstrate a wide range of vocabulary with minimal repetition.

4a. For your quinceañera or 15th birthday, your godparents have sent you to visit your grandparents who live in Mexico. Write a note of twenty words in Spanish to your godparents thanking them for the gift. You may wish to:

- Thank them for the gift
- Express your feelings about the gift
- Describe your activities at your grandparents' house
- Mention the other members of the family that live there

4b. You and your family are taking a trip to Spain this summer. Write a message in Spanish to your Spanish tour guide telling him or her about your family so that he recognizes your family when he meets you at the airport. You may wish to include:

- The date and time of your arrival
- The names of family members
- Descriptions of family members
- The color of clothing you will be wearing

4c. Your pen pal is coming to visit you this summer. He would like to know about your family. Write a note to your pen pal describing your family members. You may wish to include:

- The names of your family members
- The physical characteristics of your family members
- The personality traits of your family
- The activities your family likes to do

FAMILY LIFE

ANSWER SHEET

Nombre_____ Fecha_____

PART 1: SPEAKING (30%) _____
PART 2: LISTENING (30%)   **PART 3: READING** (20%)

	2a.		2b.		2c.		3a.(8%)		3b.(12%)
1._____		4._____		7._____		11._____		15._____
2._____		5._____		8._____		12._____		16._____
3._____		6._____		9._____		13._____		17._____
				10._____		14._____		18._____

PART 4: WRITING (20%) **20 WORDS**   **4a , 4b or 4c Write 2 paragraphs.**

1_____

_____

_____

_____

_____

_____

_____

_____

_____

2_____

_____

_____

_____

_____

_____

_____

_____

_____

_____

FAMILY LIFE

AUTHENTIC ASSESSMENT

Preparing For An International Marriage

Situation: Your cousin Roberto is planning to marry Selena Blanco, who lives in Cuernava, México.

1. To help Selena get acquainted with your family, create a written family tree of your family. Include at least ten (10) people, their names and relationship to you. (For this project, you may use your own family members and/or create family members.)

2. Based on the family tree you have created, assist Selena's mother with the wedding preparations by arranging your family's seating chart diagram for the wedding reception at a restaurant in Cuernavaca. Usual seating concerns: boy/girl, couples, age groups, children, etc. Each table holds a maximum of 6 people. It is up to you to plan the optimum arrangement of people so that everyone is pleased with their seat. If necessary, you may add more tables.

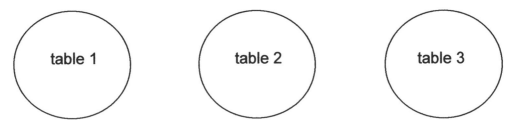

3. So that Selena's family can quickly become acquainted with your family, design a Web site or photo album based on the family you have created. Describe each family member physically, his or her personality and his or her preferences. You may use magazine/newspaper pictures or drawings instead of real photos.

4. *¡Diviértete!* The wedding day has arrived. You and your family are at Roberto's and Selena's wedding reception at the **Restaurante Maximiliano** in Cuernavaca, Mexico. Role-play with your classmates. Your classmates will play the role of Selena's mother and father. See how long and how well you can keep the conversation going in Spanish. Encourage everyone to speak by questioning the others and by adding to the conversation yourself. Each participant should think about his or her character's role in advance. Create some statements or questions that would be appropriate, or topics to bring up during the conversation.

FAMILY LIFE

Selena and Roberto's wedding (continued)

Below are helpful excerpts from Selena's letter about her family:

Mi padre, Daniel Blanco, tiene 50 años y trabaja en una compañía mejicana, Sanborns. A él le gustan los deportes del invierno, especialmente le encanta esquiar. Ganó un trofeo en Los Juegos Olímpicos cuando tenía 20 años. Con sus hermanos, él construyó la casa donde nosotros vivimos ahora.

Mi madre, Maribel Olvedo de Blanco, tiene 45 años. Ella es profesora de matemáticas en la Universidad de Cuernavaca. A ella le gustan los deportes de invierno también, pero ella no pasa mucho tiempo praticándolos porque ella tiene 4 hijos y ella trabaja también. A mi madre le encantan las fiestas tradicionales con la familia y prepara cenas magníficas.

5. Do research about Cuernavaca using the Internet or reference books:

    a. Draw a map showing the route your family will drive from the Airport in Mexico City to Cuernavaca.

    b. In order to insure a more enjoyable time with Selena's family, find out about family life in Cuernavaca. How is it the same or different from your family life? Write down your findings.

    c. Write down five places of interest your family would enjoy visiting while in Cuernavaca. In Spanish, write why you chose these places.

    d. Based on your research on the products and specialties of Cuernavaca, list five souvenirs of Cuernavaca you and your family are buying to bring home. In Spanish, write how each souvenir corresponds with the person's hobbies, interests or preferences.

    e. Write a note in Spanish to a classmate telling about your stay with Selena's family and what places you are visiting in Cuernavaca. Mention when you are returning.

House and Home

La Casa

el piso
el cuarto
el sótano
la habitación
el dormitorio
la alcoba
la cocina
el comedor
el cuarto de baño
el baño
la sala
la sala de estar
el garaje
la piscina
el techo
el jardín
la guardilla
el patio

Las Actividades

dormir
comer
cocinar
hacer la tarea
limpiar
mirar la tele
hablar por teléfono
jugar
lavar los platos
lavar la ropa
hacer
hacer la cama
poner la mesa
quitar la mesa
estudiar
escuchar música (los discos)
pasar la aspiradora
sacudir los muebles
cortar el césped

Los Muebles

el sofá
el sillón
la lámpara
el radio
la cama
el espejo
el estéreo
el juego electrónico
el lavabo / lavamanos
la ducha
la nevera
la estufa
el teléfono
el microondas
la mesa
la alfombra
la televisión
la silla
el tocador
el escritorio
la computadora
el inodoro
la bañera
el fregadero
el refrigerador
el lavaplatos
el horno
la videocasetera

Los Adjetivos

amueblado
terminado
moderno
grande
mediano
pequeño
nuevo
viejo
de ladrillo
rojo, anaranjado, amarillo, verde, azul
blanco, gris, negro

Las Expresiones

¿Dónde está(n)_____? ¿Está(n)_____ en_____?
¿Qué hace? ¿Cómo es _____?
¿De qué color es_____? ¿Quién_____?
¿Es _____ o_____?

PRE-TESTING ACTIVITIES

1. After the new vocabulary for furniture has been presented, let the students play "categories." Place the students into groups of 4. Prepare a ditto of the side view of an empty house with all of the rooms labeled in Spanish. Have all the members of the group give the assigned secretary the words in Spanish of the furniture that belongs in each room. No notes may be used. The team that comes up with the most words, wins. Afterwards, all of the students may fill in their own "charts" by placing the winning list on the blackboard or a transparency.

2. After vocabulary for the rooms of the house and the verb "*estar*" have been presented, the students may play "*El Escondite*" or "Hide and go Seek." The students pick a room to hide their dog. The other student must guess by asking, "*¿Está el perro en*_____ (a room of the house)?", until the student guesses correctly. The purpose of this activity is to reinforce vocabulary and use the verb "*estar*" for location. This exercise may also be used to review verb forms and furniture items. This game may be played as a class, in pairs or in groups of 4.

3. After the new vocabulary for the activities done in the house has been presented, the students can play "Partner Race." In this exercise, each student writes down on a piece of paper 3 activities (from a list of 20 activities) they do in a pre-selected room of the house. The objective is for each partner to guess (by asking one question at a time) what their partner has written. When one of the partners has successfully guessed all three, they may continue to see how long it takes to guess the remaining partner's answers. The partner must answer in complete sentences either affirmatively or negatively. This exercise reinforces verb forms, mainly the "*tú*" and "*yo*" forms. It also allows students to practice negative responses.

Example: Partner 1: En la sala yo...   duermo, miro la tele, etc.
Partner 1: ¿Escuchas la radio?
Partner 2: No. No escucho la radio. ¿Bailas?
Partner 1: No. No bailo. Miras la tele?
Partner 2: Sí, miro la tele. ¿Juegas?
Partner 1: etc.

HOUSE AND HOME

PRE-TESTING ACTIVITIES - continued

4. Have students decipher the abbreviations used in house ads from a Spanish newspaper, then allow them to prepare and ad about their own house.

5. The students can prepare a collage of a house and label all of the furniture. The more artistic student can draw it. The best ones can be displayed on the bulletin board.

6. Another activity for the reinforcement of activities is "La Búsqueda" or "Search." The objective is for the students to find out who does certain activities in and around the house. The teacher should prepare a list of 5 activities listed in the third person singular. Each of the students will have the same list. The students are then instructed to circulate around the room and get the signature of five different students who perform those activities. The students may only ask two questions of each student and may not get more than one signature for any one student. All questions must be asked and answered in complete Spanish sentences.

USEFUL CULTURAL CONCEPTS FOR THIS CHAPTER

• Patios are built in the center of the house.
• Apartments are very common.
• *el bidet*
• Numbering of floors, *la planta baja*

Los Refranes:
• Son muchas manos en un plato.
• No solo de pan vive el hombre.
• La mejor medicina es la buena comida.
• Casa sin madre, río sin cauce.

SCHOOL-TO-WORK

Using visuals and possibly a field trip, introduce how Spanish styles influenced the fields of architecture and architectural landscaping. Some architectural styles brought to America by the Spanish are *Baroque, Gothic, Moorish, and Romanesque.* These styles of architecture can be found in the southwestern United States (California, Texas, Arizona and New Mexico). Some examples of Spanish architectural influences are:

1. clay roofs
2. roughly plastered doors
3. colorful ceramic tile

SCHOOL-TO-WORK- continued

4. arched doorways
5. wrought iron window grills
6. patios

An example of architectural landscaping influenced by the Spanish is on the patios. These patios are landscaped with beautiful interior gardens, fountains, fireplaces and balconies.

Some possible sites to see fine examples of Spanish architecture and architectural landscaping are:

California: Los Angeles: courtyard residential buildings (patios)
Texas: San Antonio: The Alamo (architecture)
Arizona: Tuscon: The Westward Look Resort (architecture)
New Mexico: Albuquerque: The Albuquerque Museum (arched doorways)

SPEAKING SITUATIONS FOR PART 1 OF THE EXAM (30%)

1. Your family is going to host an exchange student from Chile. The student calls you on the phone to find out about your house.

2. You meet an exchange student from Argentina. Ask what his or her favorite room is and why it is his/her favorite.

3. You are thinking of renting a house in Mexico for the summer. You are on the telephone with the owner. Ask him or her about the house.

TEACHER'S SCRIPT FOR THE EXAM, PART 2 (Listening, 30%)

Part 2a Directions: For each question, you will hear some background information in English. Then you will hear a passage in Spanish twice, followed by a question in English. Listen carefully. After you have heard the question read the question and the four suggested answers. Choose the best answer and write its number in the appropriate space on your answer sheet. (9%)

1.   José is talking to his friend on the phone. His friend asks:

-¿Qué haces José?
-Lavo los platos.
-¿Por qué?
-Porque a mi papá no le gusta.

Where is José?   (4)

2. You are listening to the radio and hear this commercial.

Hola. ¿Le gusta dormir? ¿Tiene un dormitorio en su casa? Entonces, yo tengo muebles muy buenos para su dormitorio si le gusta dormir.

What does the announcer want you to do?   (4)

3. You are talking to your friend on the phone. He says:

¿Tu dormitorio es pequeño? ¿Por qué no haces la tarea en el comedor después de comer? La mesa en el comedor es grande.

What does your friend suggest you do? (4)

Part 2b Directions: For each question, you will hear some information in English. Then you will hear a passage in Spanish twice, followed by a question in Spanish. Listen carefully. After you have heard the question and the four suggested answers. Choose the best answer and write its number in the appropriate space on your answer sheet. (9%)

4. Pablo, an exchange student from Spain, is describing his home to the class. He says:

Mi casa en España tiene 3 pisos con 10 dormitorios, 4 baños, un garaje para 3 autos y un sótano para fiestas. Aquí en mi casa en__ (your town)__, hay 2 dormitorios y un baño.

¿Cómo es la casa de Pablo en España?   (4)

5. You are visiting Marco, your Spanish-speaking friend. He is showing you his room. He says:

Me gusta mi dormitorio. Es muy grande. Tengo un estéreo y muchos discos. Es bueno, ¿verdad?

¿Por qué le gusta a Marco esta habitación?   (3)

6.   Mrs. López is calling her son, Julio, on the phone from work.

        -Hola Julio, ¿Qué tal?
        -Bien, mamá?
        -¿Qué haces?
        -Pongo la mesa para comer.
        -Muy bien. Hasta luego.

        ¿Dónde está Julio?   (4)

Part 2c Directions: For each question, you will hear some background information in English. Then you will hear a passage in Spanish twice, followed by a question in English. Listen carefully. After you have heard the question, read the question and look at the 4 pictures on your test. Choose the picture that best answers the question and write its number in the appropriate space on your answer sheet. (12%)

7.   María is explaining to her teacher why she doesn't have her homework. She says:

        Señor Vásquez, siempre hago la tarea. Pero hoy no la tengo. Está en el inodoro en mi casa.

        Where is María's homework?   (4)

8.   Paco is telling his friend what he likes to do in his room. He says:

        Me gusta mucho mi dormitorio porque es grande. También tengo una cama grande donde leo. Me gusta mucho leer. Leo todos los días en mi cama.

        Which item is most likely from Paco's room?   (3)

9.   Marta is telling her friend about her father. She says:

        A mi papá le gusta comer. Su comida favorita es la hamburguesa. El hace las hamburguesas en la estufa todos los miércoles.

        Where can Marta's father be found on Wednesdays?   (2)

10. Today is Sunday and Juan is at the beach. His friend asks him where his sister is.

-Juan, ¿Dónde está María?
-Hoy es domingo. Todos los domingos mi hermana, María, limpia la nevera, el horno y el fregadero.

Where is Juan's sister? (1)

Reading Comprehension answers:

| 3 a. (8%) | 11. 3 | 12. 4 | 13. 3 | 14. 1 |
| 3 b. (12%) | 15. 1 | 16. 4 | 17. 3 | 18. 3 |

EXAMINATION

Nombre_____   Fecha_____

Part 1 SPEAKING (30%)
Part 2 LISTENING (30%)

Part 2a Directions: For each question, you will hear some background information in English. Then you will hear a passage in Spanish twice, followed by a question in English. Listen carefully. After you have heard the question, read the question and the four suggested answers. Choose the best answer and write its number in the appropriate space on your answer sheet. (9%)

1. Where is José?
    1. in the bathroom   3. in the bedroom
    2. in the dining room   4. in the kitchen

2. What does the announcer want you to do?
    1. buy a new house   3. take a nap
    2. refurnish your office   4. buy a bed

3. What does your friend suggest to you?
    1. To do your homework in the bedroom.
    2. To eat dinner in the dining room.
    3. To eat dinner in the bedroom.
    4. To do your homework in the dining room.

Part 2b Directions: For each question, you will hear some background information in English. Then you will hear a passage in Spanish twice, followed by a question in Spanish. Listen carefully. After you have heard the question, read the question and the four suggested answers. Choose the best answer and write its number in the appropriate space on your answer sheet. (9%)

4. ¿Cómo es la casa de Pablo en España?
    1. pequeña   3. verde
    2. gris   4. grande

5. ¿Por qué le gusta a Marco esta habitación?
    1. le gusta comer   3. le gusta escuchar música
    2. le gusta cocinar   4. le gusta limpiar

6. ¿Dónde está Julio?
    1. en el dormitorio   3. en el garaje
    2. en el baño   4. en el comedor

HOUSE AND HOME

Part 2c Directions: For each question, you will hear some background information in English. Then you will hear a passage in Spanish twice, followed by a question in English. Listen carefully. After you have heard the question, read the question and look at the 4 pictures on your test. Choose the picture that best answers the question and write its number in the appropriate space on your answer sheet. (12%)

7. Where is María's homework?

8. Which item is most likely from Paco's room?

9. Where can Marta's father be found on Wednesdays?

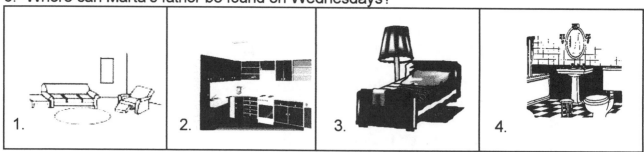

10. Where is Juan's sister?

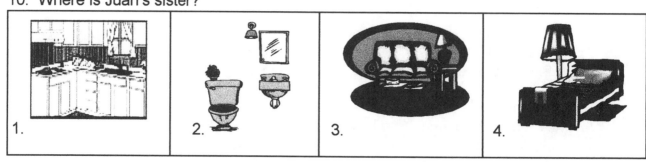

Part 3 Reading (20%)

Part 3a Directions: Answer the questions in English based on the reading selections in Spanish. Choose the best answer to each question. Base your choice on the content of the reading selection. Write the number of your answer in the appropriate space on your answer sheet. (8%)

(1)

> Madrid casa gr., dos dorm., coc. Mod., sot. term. Llame 123-4567

(3)

> Sevilla casa mod., dos pisos, cinco dorm., jard., coc. 123-0001

(2)

> Barcelona tres dorm, mod., tres baños, piscina, llame 123-4568

(4)

> Valencia un dorm., un baño, coc., aire acond., gar. 123-0002

11. According to these ads for houses in Spain, which one has the most bedrooms?
    - 1. (1)
    - 2. (2)
    - 3. (3)
    - 4. (4)

12. Which house has a place to put your car?
    - 1. (1)
    - 2. (2)
    - 3. (3)
    - 4. (4)

13. What does this ad offer?
    - 1. a boat
    - 2. a basement
    - 3. a pool
    - 4. air conditioning

14. Which room comes furnished?
    - 1. the kitchen
    - 2. the dining room
    - 3. the living room
    - 4. the bedroom

> PUERTO MAZARRON
> Costa Calida-Murcia
>
> DUPLEX Y APARTAMENTOS
> Urbanización Residencial
> Privada dotada de servicio de
> piscine, cafeteria y solarium
>
> Chimenea en la sala-comedor de
> los duplex
> Cocina amueblada, incluyendo:
> Placa de cocina-Nevera-Extracto
>
> RESA
> P. DE LA CASTELLANA, 181-8
> Tels. (91) 555 61 30 MADRID

Part 3b Directions: Answer the Spanish questions based on the reading selections in Spanish. Choose the best answer to each question. Write the number of your answer in the appropriate space on your answer sheet. (12%)

15. En el dibujo, la señora…
    1. limpia el piso.   3. limpia el techo.
    2. cocina.   4. duerme.

16. ¿Cómo es José?
    1. tonto   3. paciente
    2. generoso   4. inteligente

17. ¿Dónde pones los productos en el anuncio?
    1. En la estufa   3. En la nevera
    2. En la radio   4. En el espejo

FRIGORÍFICO
para comida fresca..

ponga los vegetales aquí

ponga la gaseosa aquí

ponga las carnes aquí

¡Qué fácil es!

18. ¿Para qué habitación son estos productos?
    1. la cocina   3. el baño
    2. la sala   4. el comedor

A G U A B U E N A
inodoros   duchas
lavabos   alfombras
   bañeras   cortinas
CALLE 30
Córdoba, Esp.
555-23-45

HOUSE AND HOME

PART 4 WRITING (20%)

Part 4a Directions: Choose two of the three writing tasks provided below. Your answer to each of the two questions should be written entirely in Spanish and should contain a minimum of **20 words**.

Place names and brand names written in Spanish count as one word. Contractions are counted as one word. Salutations, closing, and commonly used abbreviations are included in the word count. Numbers, unless written as words, and names of people do not count as words.

Be sure that you have satisfied the purpose of the task. The sentence structure and/or expressions used should be connected logically and demonstrate a wide range of vocabulary with minimal repetition.

Part 4a: You have recently moved. Write a short note in Spanish to your pen pal in Spain. Describe why you like your house. You may wish to include:

- The size of the house or apartment
- The names of the rooms
- The type and kind of furniture
- A description of the garden

Part 4b: You and your family are going to exchange houses with a family in Venezuela. Write a note to describe your bedroom in Spanish. You may wish to include the following ideas:

- The color of your room
- What activities you do in that room
- The items you have in your room
- How you feel about it

4c. Your pen pal is coming to visit you this summer. Your family has just built a new home in San Diego. Invite your friend to come to stay with you in your home. Describe the room where he or she will stay and activities you are going to do in and out side of the house.
You may wish to include:

- An invitation to visit and stay in your house
- The description of the house
- Activities to do in the house
- Activities to do outside of the house

ANSWER SHEET

Nombre_____ **Fecha**_____

PART 1: SPEAKING (30%) _____
PART 2: LISTENING (30%)   **PART 3: READING** (20%)

     2a.   2b.   2c.   3a.(8%)   3b.(12%)

1._____   4._____   7._____   11._____   15._____

2._____   5._____   8._____   12._____   16._____

3._____   6._____   9._____   13._____   17._____

                   10._____   14._____   18._____

PART 4: WRITING (20%) **20 WORDS** **4a , 4b or 4c Write 2 paragraphs.**

1_____

_____

_____

_____

_____

_____

_____

_____

_____

2_____

_____

_____

_____

_____

_____

_____

_____

_____

HOUSE AND HOME

AUTHENTIC ASSESSMENT

Exchanging Homes For The Summer

Situation: Your family would like to spend the summer in Spain and to exchange homes with a family living in Madrid.

1. Design an ad in Spanish for the Internet or a newspaper in Madrid requesting to exchange homes with a family living in Madrid. Include rooms in your home, conveniences, advantages of living in your area, and how you may be contacted.

2. Research on the Internet about Madrid and make a list of similarities and differences between Madrid and where you live.

3. A classmate will play the role of someone telephoning to answer your ad. Find out about his or her Madrid home and answer questions about your home.

4. ¡**Felicitaciones**! Your efforts have been successful and you are now living in Madrid. Based on your Madrid research and your creativity, write a note in Spanish to a classmate describing your home in Spain and what your daily routine is like.

MI CASA ES SU CASA

EDUCATION

EDUCATION

Las Asignaturas:

el alemán
el arte
el curso
el español
el francés
el horario
el italiano
el período
la clase
la economía doméstica
la educación física
la geografía
la historia
la música
las artes manuales
las ciencias
las matemáticas

Las Actividades:

abrir
aprender
asistir a
cantar
cerrar
comprender
contestar
correr
dibujar
escribir
estudiar
hablar
hacer la tarea
pintar
preguntar
sacar una buena/mala nota
tocar (un instrumento)
tomar apuntes
trabajar
ver una película

La Escuela:

el colegio
el liceo
la universidad

La Sala de Clase:

el alumno / la alumna
el baño
el cuaderno
el escritorio
el / la estudiante
el examen
el gimnasio
el laboratorio
el lápiz
el libro
el maestro / la maestra
el papel
el profesor / la profesora
el proyector
el pupitre
el tablón de anuncios
la bandera
la computadora
la película
la pizarra
la pluma
la prueba
la tarea
la tiza

Los Adjetivos:

aburrido
corto
difícil
divertido
fácil
interesante
largo
todo

Los Días de la Semana:

lunes
martes
miércoles
jueves
viernes
sábado
domingo

EDUCATION

Las Expresiones:

¿Cuándo?
¿En qué período tienes la clase de...?
¿A qué hora?
¿Qué hora es?
¿Qué haces en la clase de...?
¿Dónde está la clase de...?
¿Cuál es tu materia favorita?
¿Qué clase prefieres?
¿Quién es tu profesor preferido?

por la mañana
en la mañana
por la tarde
en la tarde
por la noche
en la noche

antes
después
hasta

los números 1-500

PRE-TESTING ACTIVITIES

1. Students write out their schedules in Spanish. The students exchange schedules in class and ask questions about them in Spanish.

2. After the new vocabulary has been taught, the students play the *Categories* game. A different course title is written in a separate box. Assign one student in each group to be the secretary. The remaining students will dictate from memory the activities done in each of the different classes. The team with the most logical activities listed wins. Afterwards, all possibilities may be written on the board or on an overhead transparency for all of the students to copy.

3. On the Internet, students study the Web sites of schools in Spanish-speaking countries and compare these schools with their own school.

4. The students draw a picture or make a diorama of a classroom and label the parts in Spanish.

EDUCATION

USEFUL CULTURAL CONCEPTS FOR THIS CHAPTER

- Comparison of the Spanish and various Latin-American school systems and requirements for graduation
- Establishment of a "sister-school" pen pal program with a school in Puerto Rico
- Review of the 24-hour clock
- Report card grades and test grades
- The implications of bilingualism on the American school system

Los Refranes:

- Cada día se aprende algo nuevo.
- Para aprender, nunca es tarde.
- Es más fácil de decir que de hacer.
- Vivir para ver, y ver para saber.
- Nada hay más atrevido que la ignorancia.

SCHOOL-TO-WORK

1. Provide a list of cognates related to education and have the students attempt to guess the meanings. Have a discussion of the importance of a strong vocabulary to the acquisition of a good job or to job advancement.

2. Have the students research jobs and compare the salaries of jobs where Spanish language skills are requested with those where they are not. Make a bulletin board of the types of jobs available in your region, which consider foreign language skills to be a bonus. In addition, list the salaries which they offer.

3. Have the students research jobs as foreign language teachers. Students will see the advantages of developing their skills beyond the basic requirements for graduation. Let students take turns "teaching" small sections of material or reviewing homework assignments.

SPEAKING SITUATIONS FOR PART 1 OF THE EXAM (30%)

1. Your friend is ill. Telephone him or her to discuss what is happening at school.

2. You and your friend are discussing some of your teachers. You disagree with his or her opinion about one of them. Discuss your reasons.

3. Your sister needs to decide whether she should take Spanish next year. Convince her to continue her study of the language.

4. The exchange student from Mexico is sitting with you in the cafeteria. Ask him about his school.

5. You are staying with a host family in Costa Rica. Your host parents want to know what an American school is like. Describe your school.

TEACHER'S SCRIPT FOR THE EXAM, PART II (Listening, 30%)

Part 2a Directions: For each question, you will hear some background information in English. Then you will hear a passage in Spanish twice, followed by the question in English. Listen carefully. After you have heard the question, read the question and the four suggested answers. Choose the best answer and write its number in the appropriate space on your answer sheet. (9%)

1. You are talking to your friend about school. He says:

   No me gusta mi clase del período dos. La profesora es simpática pero la asignatura es muy difícil. Nosotros dibujamos y pintamos, pero no me gusta dibujar y pintar.

   What should your friend do? (2)

2. Juan is talking to you about his school in Bolivia. He says:

   En Bolivia tengo seis clases. Me gustan todas, excepto las matemáticas. En mi clase favorita nosotros jugamos al fútbol. Me encanta el fútbol.

   What is Juan's favorite class? (3)

3. On the plane you are talking to a passenger who is a teacher from Mexico. She says:

   Yo soy profesora en un colegio grande en la capital. Todos mis estudiantes cantan muy bien.

   Who would enjoy taking this teacher's class? (2)

Part 2b. Directions: For each question, you will hear some background information in English. Then you will hear a passage in Spanish twice, followed by the question in English. Listen carefully. After you have heard the question, read the question and the four suggested answers on your test paper. Choose the best answer and write its number in the appropriate space on your answer sheet.

4. María is talking to you about her schedule. She says:

   Mi horario es muy difícil. Tengo la clase de ciencias el período uno, las matemáticas el período dos, la historia el período tres, el inglés el período cuatro, y el español el período cinco. No tengo el almuerzo hasta el período seis. Después, tengo el arte y la educación física.

   ¿Cómo es su horario? (3)

5. Jorge is telling you about one of his teachers. He says:

   Mi profesor de inglés es interesante. La clase es divertida también. Nosotros leemos libros y yo aprendo mucho, pero no tenemos mucha tarea. Me gusta mucho la clase de inglés.

   ¿Cómo es el profesor? (2)

6. Juan Manuel is describing his school in Chile. He says:

   Mi escuela es muy grande y vieja. Las salas son muy grandes y tienen pupitres de diferentes colores, como rojo y azul. Me gustan mucho los rojos. También hay computadoras, televisores, videocaseteras y proyectores en cada sala de clase.

   ¿Cómo son las salas de clase en el colegio en Chile? (2)

Part 2c. Directions: For each question, you will hear some background information in English. Then you will hear a passage in Spanish twice, followed by the question in English. Listen carefully. After you have heard the question, read the question and look at the four pictures on your test paper. Choose the picture that best answers the question and write its number in the appropriate space on your answer sheet.

7. You are attending a school in Puerto Rico. Your teacher says:

   Ahora vamos a estudiar las matemáticas. La lección es un poco difícil. Saquen sus libros por favor.

   What do you need from your desk? (2)

8.   You are talking with your friend, Javier, at a stationery store in Spain. He says:

Tengo una profesora nueva en mi clase de inglés. Ella es antipática y la clase es mala. Tomamos muchos apuntes y necesito comprar un cuaderno nuevo.

What should Javier buy? (1)

9.   Adela is complaining about her history teacher.
La clase del señor Rivera es muy difícil. El siempre escribe en la pizarra. Nosotros tomamos apuntes todo el período. Compro muchas plumas para esta clase.

What does the teacher use in class? (2)

10.   You are in Colombia and your friend Pedro is sick at home. You are visiting him and he wants you to deliver a note to his teacher. He asks:

Por favor, dale este papel a mi profesora. Ella es alta y gorda. Tiene el pelo rubio. Ella se llama la señorita López.

Which is Pedro's teacher? (4)

Reading Comprehension Answers:

3a. (8%)   11. (4)   12. (1)   13. (2)   14. (1)

3b. (12%)   15. (4)   16. (2)   17. (4)   18. (3)

EDUCATION

Nombre:_____ **Fecha**_____

EXAMINATION

PART 1: SPEAKING (30%)
PART 2: LISTENING (30%)

Part 2a. Directions: For each question, you will hear some background information in English. Then you will hear a passage in Spanish twice, followed by the question in English. Listen carefully. After you have heard the question, read the question and the four suggested answers on your test paper. Choose the best answer and write its number in the appropriate space on your answer sheet. (9%)

1.   What should your friend do?
       1. pursue a career in art   3. try to change teachers
       3. try to change his class   4. study harder

2.   What is Juan's favorite class?
       1. math   3. gym
       2. history   4. English

3.   Who would enjoy taking this teacher's class?
       1. someone who likes to eat   3. someone who likes to read
       2. someone interested in music   4. someone who likes to add

Part 2b. Directions: For each question, you will hear some background information in English. Then you will hear a passage in Spanish twice, followed by the question in English. Listen carefully. After you have heard the question, read the question and the four suggested answers on your test paper. Choose the best answer and write its number in the appropriate space on your answer sheet.

4.   ¿Cómo es su horario?
       1. Es malo porque no tiene almuerzo.
       2. Es bueno porque no tiene el período uno.
       3. Es malo porque no come hasta el período seis.
       4. Es bueno porque tiene arte en el período uno.

5.   ¿Cómo es el profesor?
       1. Es antipático.   3. Es estúpido.
       2. Es simpático.   4. Es aburrido.

6.   ¿Cómo son las salas de clase en el colegio en Chile?
       1. Son feas.   3. Son aburridas.
       2. Son modernas.   4. Son pequeñas.

EDUCATION

Part 2c. Directions: For each question, you will hear some background information in English. Then you will hear a passage in Spanish twice, followed by the question in English. Listen carefully. After you have heard the question, read the question and look at the four pictures on your test paper. Choose the picture that best answers the question and write its number in the appropriate space on your answer sheet.

7. What do you need from your desk?

8. What should Javier buy?

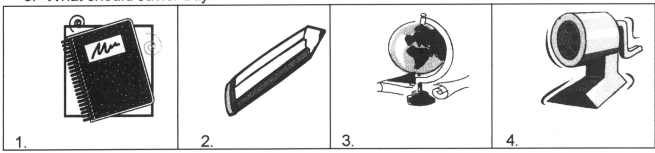

9. What does the teacher use in class?

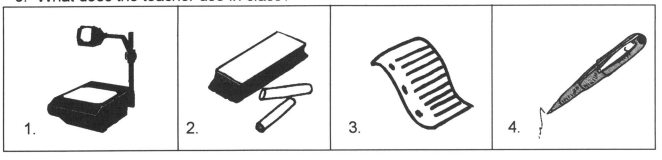

10. Which is Pedro's teacher?

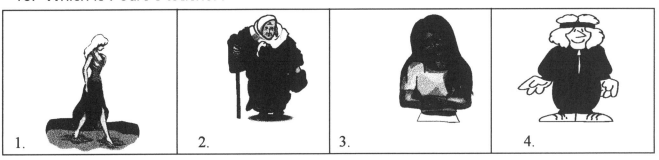

PART 3: READING (20%)

Part 3a Directions: Answer the question in English based on the reading selection in Spanish. Choose the best answer to each question. Base your choice on the content of the reading selection. Write the number of your answer in the appropriate space on your answer sheet.

(1)

Aprenda a hablar inglés fácilmente. Tenemos laboratorios y profesores muy buenos. Llámenos: 555-11-11. Esutdie los lunes-viernes 8-3:00
Escuela de Idiomas de Carácas

(2)

ESCUELA DE BUEN COMER
¿Te gusta la comida? ¿Tienes una cocina en tu casa? Esta escuela te va a enseñar a cocinar como tu mamá.
Llámanos: 555-12-12

(3)

UNIVERSIDAD DE VENEZUELA
clases de noche
Tocar el piano, la guitarra y más
Escuchar el flamenco

Matriculación: 7 noviembre

(4)

Aprenda a reparar autos, camiones y aviones en 6 semanas en ESCUELA SEAT.
Clases de lunes a jueves
Calle Colón 34, 555-13-13

11.   Which school would you attend if you wanted to be a mechanic?
        1. (1)   3. (3)
        2. (2)   4. (4)

12.   Which school would you attend if you wanted to learn a language?
        1. (1)   3. (3)
        2. (2)   4. (4)

ESCUELA SAN JOSÉ DEL CAMPO
Horario escolar

ESTUDIANTE: __José Luis García López__

Período	Asignatura	Sala	Profesor
1.	Español 8	45	Sr. Cervantes
2	Historia 8	27	Srta. Perón
3	Aula est.	10	Sr. Rivera
4	Inglés	48	Sra. Londres
5	Matemáticas 8	33	Srta. Santana
6	Almuerzo	cafetería	-------------
7	Educación física	gimnasio	Sr. Maradona
8	Música	18	Sra. Segovia

Firma del director: *María-Carmen Fuentes de Montoya*

13. Who is José's teacher for study hall?
    1. Miss Perón
    2. Mr. Rivera
    3. Mr. Maradona
    4. Mrs. Segovia

14. What subject does Mrs. Londres teach?
    1. English
    2. Spanish
    3. Industrial Arts
    4. Gym

Part 3b: Directions: Answer the questions based on the reading selections in Spanish. Choose the best answer to each question and write it's number in the appropriate space on your answer sheet.

PROFESORA MEXICANA NOMINADA "PROFESORA DEL AÑO"

México. La señorita Susana Cárdenas, de Guadalajara, México, fue nominada para recibir el premio nacional de los profesores hoy. La nominaron por petición de sus alumnos en el Colegio Bolívar en Guadalajara. Los alumnos dicen que tiene mucho talento y que les permite a los alumnos pintar y dibujar lo que quieren. Van a muchos museos y estudian muchos artistas de México y de otros países como Italia. Un alumno suyo dice "Para mí, siempre es la profesora del año".

---

15. Según este artículo, la Srta. Cárdenas es profesora de...
    1. historia
    2. italiano
    3. música
    4. arte

16. ¿Por qué quieren los alumnos que la Srta. Cárdenas sea "La Profesora Del Año"?
    1. porque viajan a Italia en el verano
    2. Ella hace la clase muy interesante y divertida.
    3. Los alumnos reciben buenas notas en su clase.
    4. porque ella está aburrida.

Librería Blasco Ibáñez

Libros de: la biología, la química, la medicina, la física, y mucho más...

Calle España 89, Lima

17. Según este anuncio, en esta tienda hay libros para la clase de...
    1. inglés
    2. historia
    3. educación física
    4. ciencias

> **BUENOS DÍAS**
> Por favor, lean estas direcciones. Saquen dos lápices y un papel.
> Es prohibido hablar con sus amigos. Tienen todo el período para
> terminar. ¡Buena suerte!

18. Este mensaje está en la pizarra porque...
    1. El profesor está ausente
    2. El profesor necesita una pluma.
    3. Hay un examen hoy.
    4. No hay clases hoy.

PART 4: WRITING (20%)

Part 4a Directions: Choose two of the three writing tasks provided below. Your answer to each of the two questions should be written entirely in Spanish and should contain a minimum of **20 words**.

Place names and brand names written in Spanish count as one word. Contractions are counted as one word. Salutations, closing, and commonly used abbreviations are included in the word count. Numbers, unless written as words, and names of people do not count as words.

Be sure that you have satisfied the purpose of the task. The sentence structure and/or expressions used should be connected logically and demonstrate a wide range of vocabulary with minimal repetition.

4a. Write a note in Spanish to a pen pal in Mexico. Tell him/her about one of your classes in school. You may wish to include:

- The subject
- Activities that you do in class
- How you feel about the class
- The materials you have for the class

4b. A student from Costa Rica will be attending your school later on this year. Write a note in Spanish to him/her describing your school. You may wish to include the following ideas:

- The classes that are offered
- The activities that are available
- Information about the students
- Information about the teachers

Part 4 Writing (continued)

4c. You are an exchange student in Costa Rica and are attending school there. You are not feeling well today and can't attend classes. Write a note to your friend telling him or her that you will not be in school today. You may wish to include the following ideas.

- Tell him or her the books that you need
- Tell him or her to write down your homework
- Tell him or her to tell your Spanish teacher that you are sick
- Tell him or her to visit you at 3:30 p.m. at your house

EDUCATION

ANSWER SHEET

Nombre_____ **Fecha**_____

PART 1: SPEAKING (30%) _____
PART 2: LISTENING (30%)   **PART 3: READING** (20%)

2a.	2b.	2c.	3a.(8%)	3b.(12%)
1._____	4._____	7._____	11._____	15._____
2._____	5._____	8._____	12._____	16._____
3._____	6._____	9._____	13._____	17._____
		10._____	14._____	18._____

PART 4: WRITING (20%) **20 WORDS   4a , 4b or 4c Write 2 paragraphs.**

1_____

_____

_____

_____

_____

_____

_____

_____

_____

_____

_____

2_____

_____

_____

_____

_____

_____

_____

_____

_____

_____

_____

EDUCATION

AUTHENTIC ASSESSMENT
Twinning Classes

Situation: Your teacher has found another Spanish class in a nearby school with which your class will twin.

1. Prepare a video or Web site in Spanish telling about your school. Include the following topics: an introduction of your class and the teacher, a description of your classroom, the courses offered at your school and after school clubs. Include an explanation of what you like and / or dislike about your school. You may prepare this video or Web site alone or with a committee. When the video or Web site is completed, it will be viewed by your twin Spanish class.

2. With your class, watch the video or look at the Web site created by your twin Spanish class. Discuss in Spanish with your class the similarities and differences between the two schools.

3. Read the letters or e-mail messages that have been written in Spanish by the members of your twin class. Choose one letter or e-mail to answer. In your letter or e-mail, be sure to include a description of your typical school day and a copy of your schedule in Spanish.

4. *¡Diviértete!* Help plan a field trip to a Spanish movie, play, etc. which your twin class will also attend. Your two classes will meet afterwards at a Spanish restaurant to have lunch and converse in Spanish. If no suitable events are available, prepare a field trip for the two classes at your school. The day's program will be distributed to all participants. The day could start with a tour of the school in Spanish, followed by performances by members of both classes, games in Spanish and/or viewing a Spanish video. The meeting could conclude with lunch. Take photos for your local newspapers.

5. Research on the Internet or in reference books about the Spanish school system. Write a report on this subject and include how the Spanish school system is different from yours. Share your findings with the class.

N.B. This chapter's situation requires actual contact with a second Spanish class for the purpose of exchanges between both groups of students.

Community and Neighborhood

El Pueblo y El Vecindario

el banco
el barrio
el hospital
el hotel
el museo
el parque
el parque zoológico
el pueblo
el semáforo
el templo
la biblioteca
la calle
la casa
la discoteca
la esquina
la estación
la iglesia
la piscina
los animales
el cine
el teatro
la plaza
el parque
el estadio
el colegio
la universidad
el aeropuerto
la playa el tigre, el elefante
el león, la llamas

Las Tiendas

el restaurante
el supermercado
el café
la casa de correos (el correo)
la panadería
la pastelería
la tienda
la carnicería

la heladería
la farmacia
la librería
la gasolinera
el centro
el almacén
el mercado
un kilo de _____
el tráfico

Las Señales de Tráfico:

alto, una vía,
curva peligrosa
prohibido estacionarse
prohibido entrar
parada de autobús

Los Medios de Transporte:

el tren
el autobús
el metro
la motocicleta
el avión
el coche, el carro, el auto
la bicicleta
a pie

Los Adjetivos:

mediano, a
pequeño,a
excitante
hermoso,a
grande
interesante
aburrido,a
rápido,a
lento,a

COMMUNITY AND NEIGHBORHOOD

Las Actividades:	**Las Expresiones Utiles:**
caminar, ir a pie	¿Cómo voy a _____?
cobrar	¿A dónde va(s)?
parar	¿Con quién va(s)
seguir	Perdón, Perdóneme
pasar	¿Dónde está_____?
preguntar	Derecho, (todo recto)
cruzar	Entre, alrededor de
pasear	Ud. es muy amable. Otra vez, por
ir de compras	favor.
ir	¿Cómo va(s)? a _____?
subir	¿Cuándo va(s) ?
continuar	conmigo, contigo
andar	Camine a dos cuadras.
ver	A la derecha, a la izquierda
pedir	Lejos de, cerca de
dar un paseo	Enfrente de, entre
viajar	Detrás de
nadar	Lo siento.

PRE-TESTING ACTIVITIES

1. After creating a vocabulary list of places in your town, make an overhead transparency of an imaginary town. Students should be able to discern the types of buildings from the drawing. Describe something you intend to do in the town, and then ask if the students know where you are going. e.g. *Yo quiero ver la película "Los Tres Amigos", ¿A dónde voy?* Then have the students try to engage the class in the same way. For homework or during class, the students can create a map of their town including buildings, streets and their homes.

2. Using the same overhead as in number 1, the teacher can explain how to get from one place in the town to the other. The students can make a list of directions first, then the teacher can give a sample of giving directions. For example:
Person A: *Éstoy en el teatro. ¿Cómo voy al hospital?*
Person B: *Pase el cine. Continúe derecho dos cuadras. Doble a la derecha.*
Next the teacher can ask students to give him or her directions for practice. Finally, the students can use the maps they created for homework and take turns giving directions to their conversation partners. (Work in pairs.)

3. As a follow-up the students may be given a new map of a city to look at as the teacher dictates directions from one location to another. Students must give the destination. For homework the students write one or two sets of directions to be dictated the next day to his or her conversation partner.

COMMUNITY AND NEIGHBORHOOD

4. The students may take turns pretending to be lost. In pairs, using a map, one student will say to another: *Perdón, ¿Cómo voy a _____?* The second student will give directions. Then they may reverse roles.

5. If the class is not too large, the classroom can be turned into a town with desks labeled as places in the community. The students can take turns giving directions and following directions to places in the town.

6. Compare and contrast the design plan of a typical Spanish or Hispanic town to your town. You may use a Venn Diagram for this purpose.

USEFUL CULTURAL CONCEPTS FOR THIS CHAPTER

♦ The almacén; *El Corte Inglés*
♦ The peseta in Spain, and its replacement with the euro. Refer to the table of contents for further information on the euro.
♦ Cities in your country with Spanish names
♦ Map of a Spanish town; compare it with your town or city.
♦ The plaza is the center of a Hispanic town.
♦ The *corrida de toros* is located in many Spanish towns and cities. As the national pastime of Spain, it is viewed as an artistic, theatrical event.
♦ The prestige of the *torero* as a national hero
♦ La Feria de San Fermín in Pamplona and other famous festivals
♦ The influence of the Moslems especially in southern Spain
♦ Introduce Hispanic cities using the Internet, videos, maps, and reference books.

Los Refranes:

• Año de nieves, año de bienes.
• El que roba un ladrón tiene cien años de perdón.
• En el país de los ciegos, el tuerto es rey.
• El martes, ni te cases ni te embarques.
• Todos los caminos conducen a Roma.

SCHOOL - TO - WORK

1. Role-play, in Spanish, a town employee (e.g. police officer, tour guide, museum personnel, etc.) assisting a Spanish-speaking visitor in your town. List with the students in your class other town employees who would benefit from speaking Spanish; for example, sales personnel, international buyer for a department store, lawyer, receptionist, doctor, etc.

2. Discuss how Spanish would be useful to our nation's head -of-state, members of the diplomatic corps and Peace Corps volunteers.

COMMUNITY AND NEIGHBORHOOD

SPEAKING SITUATIONS FOR PART I OF THE EXAM (30%)

1. You are traveling through Spain on vacation. You are in Madrid and need directions to your hotel from the airport. Greet a policeman and ask for help.

2. Your cousin is coming to visit you from Mexico. He is planning to live in the United States and is deciding where to settle. Try to convince him to live in your town.

3. You have been asked to show relatives from Costa Rica your neighborhood. Tell them what you do in your town and why you like to live there.

4. Your are riding on a plane and you are sitting next to a Spanish teenager. Socialize by discussing and asking and answering questions about your towns.

TEACHER'S SCRIPT FOR THE EXAM, PART II (Listening, 30%)

Part 2a Directions: For each question, you will hear some background information in English. Then you will hear a passage in Spanish twice, followed by the question in English. Listen carefully. After you have heard the question, read the question and the four suggested answers. Choose the best answer and write its number in the appropriate space on your answer sheet. (9%)

1. The Ramos family is making plans for Sunday. Sara, the daughter says:

    Papá quiero ir a ver animals. Me gustan las llamas y los elefantes y también los tigres.

    Where is the family going? (4)

2. Juan, Pedro and Carlos are planning their evening. Juan says

    Pedro, ¿A dónde vamos esta noche?
    - Yo quiero mirar una película.
    - Yo también. ¿A qué hora vamos?
    - A las ocho.

    What are the boys going to do this evening? (3)

3.   Two friends are talking about what they are going to do. One says:

- Hola, Miguel ¿Cómo estás?
- Así, así. ¿Qué haces esta tarde?
- Yo voy a un restaurante con mi familia para comer la cena. Es el cumpleaños
  de mi hermana, Ana.

How is the boy celebrating his sister's birthday? (2)

Part 2b Directions: For each question, you will hear some background information in English. Then you will hear a passage in Spanish twice, followed by the question in Spanish. Listen carefully. After you have heard the question, read the question and the four suggested answers. Choose the best answer and write its number in the appropriate space on your answer sheet. (9%)

4.   You are in your town. You meet a stranger with a suitcase who says:

Perdón. ¿Cómo voy al hospital?
Ah, el hospital está muy cerca de aquí. Camine dos calles. Está a la derecha.

¿Cómo va la persona al hospital? (2)

5.   Lola's friend is telling her what she must do this afternoon. She says:

-Lola, yo tengo mucha tarea esta noche y un proyecto grande. Yo necesito libros y enciclopedias para información . Voy a la biblioteca por dos horas esta tarde.

¿Qué hace la amiga de Lola? (1)

6.   You are listening to the radio and hear this announcement.

Un día, solamente, un día, el conjunto musical "Maná" va a visitar nuestro pueblo. Santa Cruz es muy afortunado que estos jóvenes van a dar un concierto, el 2 de noviembre.

¿Cómo se llama el pueblo? (4)

Part 2c Directions: For each question, you will hear some background information in English. Then you will hear a passage in Spanish twice, followed by the question in English. Listen carefully. After you have heard the question, read the question and look at the four pictures. Choose the best answer and write its number in the appropriate space on your answer sheet. (12%)

7.   You are a student in an elementary school. Your teacher makes this announcement:

Los niños que viven lejos de las escuela, por favor, suban el autobús ahora.

Which picture is being described? (3)

8.   You are on a trip and you hear this announcement.

Todas las personas que van a España a las siete, por favor aborden el avión número 34.

Where are you? (1)

9.   You and your brother are talking about your plans for this afternoon. He says:

Hace calor hoy. Yo quiero ir a la piscina esta tarde porque me gusta nadar y hay muchas chicas bonitas.

Where is he going? (1)

10.   While traveling in Spain, a stranger asks you for directions. He says:

-Perdóname señor, ¿cómo voy a la plaza de toros? Hay una corrida a la una y tengo un boleto para un asiento en la sombra.

Where does he want to go? (4)

Reading Comprehension Answers:

3 a. (8%)	11. 2	12. 2	13. 1	14. 2
3 b. (12%)	15. 4	16. 2	17. 1	18. 3

COMMUNITY AND NEIGHBORHOOD

Nombre _____ la fecha _____

EXAMINATION

PART 1   SPEAKING (30%)
PART 2   LISTENING (30%)

Part 2a Directions: For each question, you will hear some background information in English. Then you will hear a passage in Spanish twice, followed by the question in English. Listen carefully. After you have heard the question, read the question and the four suggested answers. Choose the best answer and write its number in the appropriate space on your answer sheet. (9%)

1. Where is the family going?
   1. the airport   3. the movies
   2. the library   4. the zoo

2. What are the boys going to do this evening?
   1. swim in the pool   3. go to the movies
   2. go to the park   4. eat at a restaurant

3. How is the boy celebrating his sister's birthday?
   1. There is a party in his house.   3. They are going to the theater.
   2. They are going to a restaurant.   4. They are going to a bullfight.

Part 2b Directions: For each question, you will hear some background information in English. Then you will hear a passage in Spanish twice, followed by the question in Spanish. Listen carefully. After you have heard the question, read the question and the four suggested answers. Choose the best answer and write its number in the appropriate space on your answer sheet. (9%)

4. ¿Cómo va la persona al hospital?
   1. Toma una motocicleta.   3. Toma un tren.
   2. Va a pie.   4. Toma un avión

5. ¿Qué hace la amiga de Lola?
   1. Estudia en la biblioteca.   3. Visita con amigos.
   2. Viaja en avión.   4. Habla por teléfono.

6. ¿Cómo se llama el pueblo?
   1. Santa Fe   3. Santa Mónica
   2. Santo Domingo   4. Santa Cruz

Part 2c Directions: For each question, you will hear some background information in English. Then you will hear a passage in Spanish twice, followed by a question in English. Listen carefully. After you have heard the question, read the question and look at the 4 pictures on your test. Choose the picture that best answers the question and write its number in the appropriate space on your answer sheet. (12%)

7. Which picture is being described?

1.   2.   3.   4.

8. Where are you?

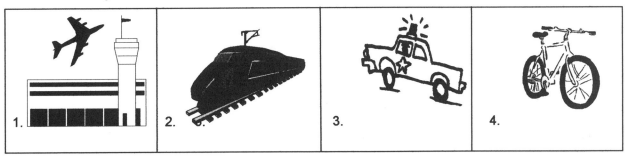

1.   2.   3.   4.

9. Where is he going?

1.   2.   3.   4.

10. Where does he want to go?

1.   2.   3.   4.

PART 3 READING (20%)

Part 3a Directions: Answer the English questions based on a reading selections in Spanish. Choose the best answer to each question. Base your choice on the content of the reading selections. Write the number of your answer in the appropriate space on your answer sheet. (8%)

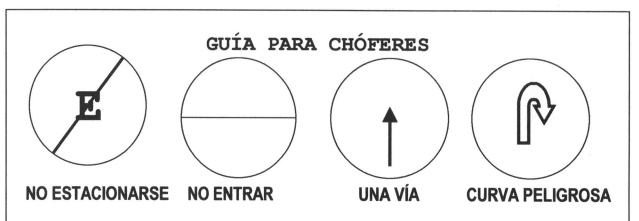

GUÍA PARA CHÓFERES

NO ESTACIONARSE   NO ENTRAR   UNA VÍA   CURVA PELIGROSA

Estas señales son muy importantes para chóferes.
Es necesario obedecerlas para hacerse un buen chófer.

11. Which sign means "Do not enter"?
   1. (1)   3. (3)
   2. (2)   4. (4)

12. Who would be interested in this information?
   1. a new mechanic   3. a dietician
   2. a new driver   4. a new chef

IXTAPA
El Paraíso   **de México**

Un pueblo pequeño con una atmósfera limpia y buena.

NATACIÓN      ÁRBOLES Y FLORES
COMIDA SABROSA   ARTE Y MÚSICA

13. Who would be interested in this ad?
    1. a traveler
    2. a bicyclist
    3. a person looking for the bank
    4. a detective

14. What does Ixtapa have to offer?
    1. department stores
    2. restaurants
    3. a big university
    4. a zoo

Part 3b Directions: Answer the Spanish questions based on a reading selections in Spanish. Choose the best answer to each question. Base your choice on the content of the reading selections. Write the number of your answer in the appropriate space on your answer sheet. (12%)

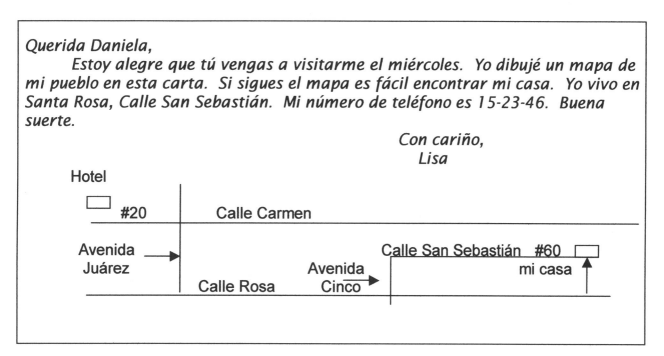

Querida Daniela,

Estoy alegre que tú vengas a visitarme el miércoles. Yo dibujé un mapa de mi pueblo en esta carta. Si sigues el mapa es fácil encontrar mi casa. Yo vivo en Santa Rosa, Calle San Sebastián. Mi número de teléfono es 15-23-46. Buena suerte.

Con cariño,
Lisa

Hotel
#20   Calle Carmen

Avenida Juárez   Calle San Sebastián #60
                   mi casa

Calle Rosa   Avenida Cinco

15. ¿Por qué escribió la carta Lisa?
    1. Es el cumpleaños de Daniela.
    2. Daniela está en Francia.
    3. Daniela está en el hospital
    4. Daniela viene a su casa.

16. Según el mapa, la dirección de Lisa es
    1. Avenida Cinco #60
    2. Calle San Sebastián #60
    3. Calle Carmen #20
    4. Avenida Juárez #20

ATENCIÓN

AFICIONADOS

DE

MANOLETE

**Es el torero más
Famoso del mundo**

a las tres
Domingo el 3 de mayo

PLAZA MAYOR   MADRID

17. ¿Qué pasa el 3 de mayo?
    1. una corrida de toros
    2. una exposición de arte
    3. un partido de fútbol
    4. un espectáculo del teatro

18. ¿Por qué es famoso Manolete?
    1. Es actor.
    2. Es torero muy conocido.
    3. Es jugador de fútbol.
    4. Es artista.

PART 4 WRITING (20%)

Part 4a Directions: Choose two of the three writing tasks provided below. Your answer to each of the two questions should be written entirely in Spanish and should contain a minimum of **20 words**.

Place names and brand names written in Spanish count as one word. Contractions are counted as one word. Salutations, closing, and commonly used abbreviations are included in the word count. Numbers, unless written as words, and names of people do not count as words.

Be sure that you have satisfied the purpose of the task. The sentence structure and/or expressions used should be connected logically and demonstrate a wide range of vocabulary with minimal repetition.

4a. For your quinceañera or 15th birthday, your godparents have sent you to a little town in Spain where your family comes from. Write a note of twenty words in Spanish to your godparents describing the town. You may wish to include:

- The name of the town
- The size of the town
- The weather
- Physical features
- Things that you do there/places to go for fun

4b. Write a message in Spanish to your Spanish key-pal telling him or her about one or more of your favorite places in your town. You may wish to include:

- The name(s) and description(s) of the place(s)
- Whom you go with
- Why you go there
- When you go there

4c. Your pen pal is coming to visit you this summer. Your town in New Mexico is having a festival honoring its saint. Write a note to your pen pal describing events during that week. You may wish to include:

- The name of the saint (Name of the town)
- The activities available
- The days of the festival
- The food you will eat

COMMUNITY AND NEIGHBORHOOD
ANSWER SHEET

Nombre_____ **Fecha**_____

PART 1: SPEAKING (30%) _____
PART 2: LISTENING (30%)

PART 3: READING (20%)

2a.	2b.	2c.
1._____	4._____	7._____
2._____	5._____	8._____
3._____	6._____	9._____
		10._____

3a.(8%)   3b.(12%)

11._____   15._____
12._____   16._____
13._____   17._____
14._____   18._____

PART 4: WRITING (20%) **20 WORDS** **4a , 4b or 4c Write 2 paragraphs.**

1_____

_____

_____

_____

_____

_____

_____

_____

_____

2_____

_____

_____

_____

_____

_____

_____

_____

_____

_____

AUTHENTIC ASSESSMENT

Introducing Sister Cities

Situation: Your town has joined the Sister City Program. Your town's sister city will be Salamanca, Spain.

1. Design in Spanish, the official brochure or Internet site about your town, which will enable your sister city's population to know your town better. Include a labeled map and description of shopping areas, recreation centers and homes. Add information about municipal leaders. Your town has also asked you to write an introductory note expressing your town's pleasure to be *"la ciudad similar"* of Salamanca and desire to learn much from this beautiful city and its people.

2. *¡Bienvendio!* A town official from Salamanca is telephoning to request information about your town in preparation fro his or her visit to your town. Answer, in Spanish, his or her questions about the features of your town, activities your town is planning during his or her visit, where and with whom he or she will stay and the best means of transportation to your town. Role-play this conversation with a classmate. Be sure to have created a schedule of activities in advance for your guest.

3. Research on the Internet and or in reference books about Salamanca and share your findings with the class:

   a. Prepare a summary of the major features of Salamanca, its history, climate, and principle industries.

   b. Locate Salamanca on a map of Spain. Indicate the route by plane from your town to Salamanca. The plane will first land in Madrid.

4. Prepare a fact-sheet of similarities and differences between Salamanca and your town. Your fact-sheet should be helpful and of interest to someone from your town who would be traveling to Salamanca.

N.B. This situation is continued in the next chapter, Meal Taking, Food and Drink.

Food and Meal Taking

FOOD AND MEAL TAKING

Las Comidas:

el desayuno
el almuerzo
la comida
la merienda
la cena

Las Actividades:

cocinar
comer
hacer
preparar
tomar

Las Expresiones:

¿A qué hora toma Ud._____?
¿A qué hora tomas_____?
¿Quién prepara_____?
¿Cuándo come Ud.?
¿Cuándo comes?
¿Qué comes para_____?

El Cubierto:

el azúcar
la cuchara
la cucharita
el cuchillo
el mantel
la mesa
la pimienta
el plato
el platillo
la sal
la servilleta
el tenedor
el vaso

Las Actividades:

poner la mesa
recoger la mesa

Las Expresiones:

a la derecha
a la izquierda
al lado de
debajo de
encima de

Las Frutas:
las fresas
el limón
la manzana
el melón
la naranja
la pera
la piña
el plátano
la sandía
la toronja

Las Legumbres:
el arroz
el bróculi, brécol
la cebolla
los frijoles
los guisantes
las judías verdes
el maíz
las papas
el pimiento
el tomate
las zanahorias

Los Alimentos:

el biftec
el bocadillo
la carne
el chocolate
los dulces
la ensalada
las galletas
la hamburguesa

FOOD AND MEAL TAKING

el helado
el jamón
la mantequilla
el pan
el perrito caliente
el pescado
el pollo
el puerco
el sándwich
la sopa
la ternera
la torta

Los Refrescos:

el agua
las bebidas
el café
el chocolate
la cerveza
la gaseosa
la leche
la limonada
la sangría
el té
el vino

El Restaurante:

bien asado
el camarero
la camarera
el mesero
la mesera
el cliente
la cuenta
el entremés
medio asado
el menú
el plato principal
poco asado
el postre
la propina

Las Actividades:
beber
ordenar
querer
recomendar
tomar

Las Expresiones:

¿En qué puedo servirle?
¡Buen provecho!
¡Qué delicioso!
Aquí tiene Ud.
¿Cuánto cuesta?
tener sed

- Quisiera_____
- Me gustaría
¡Qué sabroso!
El plato del día
Tener hambre
¿Cuál es su (tu) _____ favorito

PRE-TESTING ACTIVITIES

1. Students make a collage of their favorite foods and label them. Then in pairs, they ask each other in Spanish what their favorite foods are.

2. The teacher uses real silverware (or plastic) and directs a student volunteer to set and unset a table in front of the class. Then the teacher breaks the class up into groups of four or six and has the students practice giving commands to another student in the group to set and unset a table.

3. In groups of four the students can do the categories activity. The teacher distributes copies of a grid with five different food groups listed in Spanish and assigns one person in each group to be the secretary. The objective is for the remaining three students in the group to come up with as many foods as they can, in Spanish, that fit into those five food groups without using their notes. The team that comes up with the greatest number of correct items wins.

4. The students create an imaginary restaurant and prepare a menu with prices. This is done individually, in pairs or groups. The menus are then displayed in the classroom.

5. Several student groups prepare a list of the different foods they like and dislike. Students then create a survey of food preferences, which are photocopied and distributed to the class. Students tabulate their classmates' results and make a chart or graph to share with the class. This may be done as an extra credit or as an in-class project.

6. Students act out a scene in a restaurant, playing the different roles. This is to be performed in front of the class and/or videotaped.

7. On the Internet, students read Web sites of various Hispanic restaurants. Compare the dishes with what is commonly served in your area.

8. Prepare a Hispanic dish, possibly in conjunction with your schools' Home and Careers Department.

USEFUL CULTURAL CONCEPTS FOR THIS CHAPTER

- Specialties of regional Hispanic cuisine
- Ex. flan and paella
- Hours for meals
- Tex-Mex food

Los Refranes

- A buen hambre no hay pan duro.
- Muchas manos en un plato siempre causan arrebato.
- Se me hace la boca agua.
- La manzana podrida pierde a su compañía.
- De la mano a la boca se pierde la sopa.
- La major salsa es el hambre.

FOOD AND MEAL TAKING

SCHOOL-TO-WORK

- In class, list Spanish words pertaining to the culinary arts professions which are also used in English, e.g. *taco, burrito, enchilada, tortilla, arroz con pollo, quesadillas, jalapeños, picante, salsa, paella, gazpacho, churros, flan*, etc.

- Organize a field trip to a Spanish/Mexican restaurant for a meal and arrange in advance for the chef or other personnel to talk to the students about their work. An alternate possibility is to invite a chef to your class to speak about his/her profession.

SPEAKING SITUATIONS FOR PART 1 OF THE EXAM (30%)

1. While on vacation in Spain, you and your family go to a restaurant for dinner. Tell the waiter what you and your family would like to order.

2. You are preparing a dinner with your Spanish-speaking friend. Socialize by discussing table settings and meal preparation.

3. You are touring Mexico with friends. Your friends would like to go to an American restaurant. Convince them to go to a Mexican restaurant.

4. You are in the cafeteria talking to your Puerto Rican friend about the different foods you like and dislike.

TEACHER'S SCRIPT FOR THE EXAM, PART II (Listening, 30%)

Part 2a. Directions: For each question, you will hear some background information in English. Then you will hear a passage in Spanish twice, followed by the question in English. Listen carefully. After you have heard the question, read the question and the four suggested answers on your test paper. Choose the best answer and write its number in the appropriate space on your answer sheet.

1. You are ordering dinner in a Spanish restaurant with your friend Rosa. She says:

   Primero, quisiera la sopa de cebolla, luego un biftec, medio asado con patatas fritas. Para beber, quiero un agua mineral sin gas.

   What vegetable does Rosa order? (1)

2. Manuel, your friend from Spain, is telling you about breakfast in his country. He says:

A las 7 de la mañana tomamos un desayuno pequeño. Solo tomamos café o jugo con pan tostado, mantequilla y mermelada. No tomamos huevos y tocino como aquí en Los Estados Unidos..

What does Manuel say about breakfast? (1)

3. You have been invited to dinner at your friend, Luis', house. He says:

Después de comer, recogemos la mesa. Yo pongo los platos en la cocina y tú pones el mantel de papel y las servilletas de papel en la basura.

What should you do now? (4)

Part 2b. Directions: For each question, you will hear some background information in English. Then you will hear a passage in Spanish twice, followed by the question in Spanish. Listen carefully. After you have heard the question, read the question and the four suggested answers on your test paper. Choose the best answer and write its number in the appropriate space on your answer sheet.

4. You are listening to a Spanish radio station, and you hear this ad.

¿Está Ud. cansado? Entonces compre Café Ojo-Abierto. Le despierta por la mañana. Cómprelo en su supermercado favorito.

Este es un anuncio para….. (2)

5. While at your friend Pablo's house, his mother is about to leave, she says:

Ahora voy al supermercado. Necesito unas naranjas, unas manzanas, unas uvas, y una sandía. Luego voy a hacer una ensalada para ustedes.

¿Por qué va al supermercado la mamá de Pablo? (1)

6.   You are at a supermarket in Peru, and you hear this special announcement over the loudspeaker.

Atención. Anuncio el especial del día. Ahora hay precios bajos en todos los helados, las galletas, los pasteles y las tortas en el supermercado.

Estos productos son...... (3)

Part 2c. Directions: For each question, you will hear some background information in English. Then you will hear a passage in Spanish twice, followed by the question in Spanish. Listen carefully. After you have heard the question, read the question and look at the four pictures on your test paper. Choose the picture that best answers the question and write its number in the appropriate space on your answer sheet.

7.   You are in an Argentine restaurant. The waitress tells you about today's specials. She says:

Buenas noches. Los platos del día son el biftec a la parilla, el arroz con pollo y las hamburguesas con queso.

Which of the following meals is not a special? (1)

8.   You are talking to your friend, Raúl, in the kitchen. He says:

Tengo hambre. Voy a prepararme un taco. Tengo la lechuga, los tomates, la carne y las cebollas. Pero lo que no tengo es el queso. Voy al supermercado ahora para comprarlo.

What ingredient is Raúl missing? (1)

9.   You are at a party at your friend Alicia's house. She says:

Hola, ¿Tienes hambre? Tengo mucha comida. Compré las papas fritas, la sandía, y los perritos calientes. Yo te recomiendo el pastel de chocolate. Yo lo preparé.

What did Alicia make for the party? (4)

10.   Carlos and his friends, David y Margarita, are planning a picnic for this weekend. Carlos says:

Bueno, para el picnic este sábado, David trae el mantel, los platos y las tazas. Margarita trae los refrescos y la comida. You traigo las servilletas y el postre.

What is Carlos bringing to the picnic? (1)

Reading Comprehension answers;

3a (8%)	11.2	12.2	13.3	14.2
3b (12%)	15. 2	16.3	17.1	18.2

FOOD AND MEAL TAKING

Nombre_____ Fecha_____
EXAMINATION
PART I. SPEAKING (30%)
PART 2. LISTENING (30%)

2a. Directions: For each question, you will hear some background information in English. Then you will hear a passage in Spanish twice, followed by the question in English. Listen carefully. After you have heard the question, read the question and the four suggested answers on your test paper. Choose the best answer and write its number in the appropriate space on your answer sheet.

1. What vegetable does Rosa order?
    1. onions   3. carrots
    2. beans   4. tomatoes

2. What does Manuel say about breakfast?
    1. breakfast in the U.S. is bigger than breakfast in Spain.
    2. they don't eat breakfast in Spain.
    3. breakfast in Spain is bigger than breakfast in the U.S.
    4. butter is better than margarine.

3. What should you do now?
    1. Help cook dinner   3. Help set the table
    2. Wash the dishes   4. Help clear the table

2b. Directions: For each question, you will hear some background information in English. Then you will hear a passage in Spanish twice, followed by the question in Spanish. Listen carefully. After you have heard the question, read the question and the four suggested answers on your test paper. Choose the best answer and write its number in the appropriate space on your answer sheet.

4 Este es un anuncio para....
    1. una carne   3. una fruta
    2. una bebida   4. un supermercado

5. ¿Por qué va al supermercado la mamá de Pablo?
    1. quiere comprar frutas   3. tiene hambre
    2. no hay legumbres en casa   4. Para comprar unos jugos

6. Estos productos son...
    1. legumbres   3. postres
    2. carnes   4. bebidas

2c. Directions: For each question, you will hear some background information in English. Then you will hear a passage in Spanish twice, followed by the question in Spanish. Listen carefully. After you have heard the question, read the question and look at the four pictures on your test paper. Choose the picture that best answers the question and write its number in the appropriate space on your answer sheet.

7. Which of the following meals is not a special?

8. What is Raúl missing?

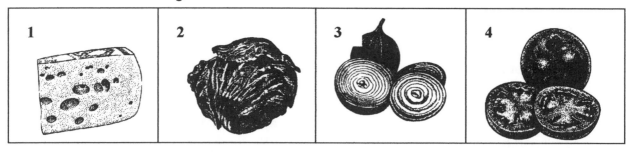

9. What did Alicia make for the party?

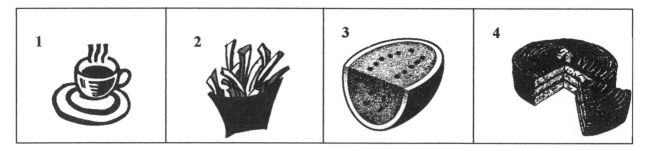

10. What is Carlos bringing to the picnic?

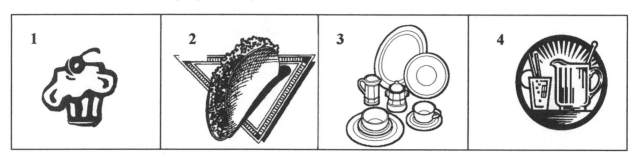

FOOD AND MEAL TAKING

Part 3a. Directions: Answer the questions in English based on the reading selections in Spanish. Choose the best answer to each question. Base your choice on the content of the reading selection. Write the number of your answer in the appropriate space on your answer sheet.

Restaurante El Pequeño México
El menú

| Calle Diana,18 |
| Veracruz, Méx. |
| 555-64-22 |

Tacos (carne).....750 pesos   enchiladas (carne).....3500 pesos
    (pollo)......1000 pesos   (pollo) .....3750 pesos
                           (queso)....2000 pesos

burritos (carne)...2500 pesos   fajitas (carne)....3500 pesos

todas las comidas se sirven con una ensalada
*la propina está incluída

---

3. According to this menu, which statement is true?
   1. Items made with cheese are more expensive.
   2. Beef items are cheaper than chicken items.
   3. Chicken items are cheaper than beef items.
   4. There is no difference in the prices.

4. If you went to this restaurant, it would be important to know that....
   1. Salad costs extra.   3. They do not serve salad
   2. The tip is already added.   4. You should leave a big tip.

1

Café Córdoba
Comidas típicas de
España

Lunes-domingo
Abierto 8-12 de la
noche
Calle Bolívar, 5
Reservaciones
555-65-17

2

Restaurante
Rodríguez

Abierto para el
almuerzo

martes a domingo

Paseo Perón, 34
555-98-98

3

Restaurante La Cucaracha

Se sirve el desayuno todos los
días de las 7-11 de la mañana
Avenida Viernes, 13
555-13-13

5. Which of the above restaurants offers breakfast?
   1. (1)   2. (2)   3. (3)   4. None of the above

6. Which restaurant is closed on Monday?
   1. (1)   2. (2)   3. (3)   4. None of the above

Part 3b. Directions: Answer the questions based on the reading selections in Spanish. Choose the best answer to each question and write the number in the appropriate space on your answer sheet.

¡AHORRE DINERO ESTE LUNES!
En Supermercado Delujo   Avenida Sandía, 9

69 pesos por kilo | 39 pesos por kilo | 59 pesos por kilo

el pan: 29 pesos cada uno
¡Sólo 1 día! El 19 de febrero

¡Vengan Aquí!

15. Según este anuncio, ¿Cuánto cuesta un kilo de cerezas?
    1. veintinueve pesos   3. diecinueve pesos
    2. sesenta y nueve pesos   4. cincuenta y nueve pesos

16. ¿Cuándo es "el especial" en este supermercado?
    1. el nueve   3. el diecineuve
    2. el veinte y nueve   4. el cincuenta y nueve

La Casa de Cristal celebra el día de las madres

Todo tiene un descuento de 30%. Cristales para el vino o la leche

Avda./Vidrio, 9
Lima 555-99-99

Te amo

17. Este anuncio es bueno si tu mamá necesita....
    1. vasos   3. platos
    2. refrescos   4. tazas

18. ¿Para qué son los productos en el anuncio?
    1. comer   3. cocinar
    2. beber   4. leer

PART 4 WRITING (20%)

Part 4a Directions: Choose two of the three writing tasks provided below. Your answer to each of the two questions should be written entirely in Spanish and should contain a minimum of **20 words**.

Place names and brand names written in Spanish count as one word. Contractions are counted as one word. Salutations, closing, and commonly used abbreviations are included in the word count. Numbers, unless written as words, and names of people do not count as words.

Be sure that you have satisfied the purpose of the task. The sentence structure and/or expressions used should be connected logically and demonstrate a wide range of vocabulary with minimal repetition.

4a. It is your birthday. Write a note to your friend in New Mexico inviting him or her to your home to attend your birthday dinner with your family. You may wish to include:

- The date of the dinner
- The address of your house
- The food you will serve
- The type of dessert you will have.

4b. Write a message in Spanish to your Costa Rican key-pal telling him or her about some of your favorite foods. Ask about his or her favorite foods. You may wish to include:

- The items you eat for breakfast
- The items you eat for lunch
- The items you eat for snack
- The items you eat for dinner
- The time of the meals
- Ask what he or she likes to eat.

4c. Your pen pal is coming to visit you this summer. Your street in Texas is having a block party. Write a note to your pen pal describing events that will happen at the party and the food each family will bring. You may wish to include:

- The date of the block party
- The activities you will do on that day
- The type of foods people will bring or make
- The food you prefer to eat

FOOD AND MEAL TAKING

ANSWER SHEET

Nombre_____ **Fecha**_____

PART 1: SPEAKING (30%) _____
PART 2: LISTENING (30%)   **PART 3: READING** (20%)

2a.	2b.	2c.	3a.(8%)	3b.(12%)
1._____	4._____	7._____	11._____	15._____
2._____	5._____	8._____	12._____	16._____
3._____	6._____	9._____	13._____	17._____
		10._____	14._____	18._____

PART 4: WRITING (20%) **20 WORDS** **4a , 4b or 4c** **Write 2 paragraphs.**

1_____

_____

_____

_____

_____

_____

_____

_____

_____

2_____

_____

_____

_____

_____

_____

_____

_____

_____

FOOD AND MEAL TAKING

AUTHENTIC ASSESSMENT

Creating a Spanish-style dinner

Situation: Town officials from Valencia, Spain, your town's sister city, will shortly arrive in your town for a week's stay. One of the week's activities will be a Spanish-style dinner. At this dinner, the food and atmosphere of Spain will be re-created in order to emphasize your town's welcome to its guests, and also to give your town's people a greater appreciation of Spain.

1. *¡Buen provecho!* Using the Internet, reference books and cookbooks, prepare a Spanish menu featuring the specialties of Spain. Decorate the classroom to suggest a Spanish motif. Continue this theme by sketching what the servers will wear to suggest Spain. Write down three different items to be placed in the dining room for decoration, which will also add an *ambiente español.*

2. In order to entice your school's Hispanic students to attend this event, give a talk in Spanish to convince them to purchase a dinner ticket. To stimulate their interest further, choose one of your menu's hot dishes and, using props or pictures, show its ingredients and narrate as you demonstrate the main steps in preparing the dish.

3. To ensure this dinner's success, compile a fact sheet for your class about Spanish eating customs and table manners. Consult research materials, class notes, and if possible, interview people who have visited or lived in Spain. On your fact sheet, mention a minimum of five items you think are important and/or of interest

Shopping

SHOPPING

La Ropa:

los pantalones
los blue jeans
la corbata
el abrigo
el cinturón
el suéter
la blusa
el vestido
los tacones
el collar
el anillo
la pulsera
las gafas   (de sol)
el pañuelo
los guantes
la gorra
el paraguas
los calzoncillos
maleta

la camisa
la camiseta
los calcetines
la chaqueta
la cartera
el pijama
el bolso
la falda
la sandalia
los aretes
los anteojos
el reloj
la ropa interior
la bufanda
el traje de baño
las botas
el impermeable
el sostén
el camisón

Los Colores:

amarillo
blanco
marrón
pardo
rosado
verde
de oro
claro

azul
gris
negro
rosa
rojo
violeta
de plata
oscuro

La Tienda:

la caja
el/la empleado, a
el departamento
gratis
la talla
el precio

el/la cajero, a
el/la cliente, a
la ganga
el/la camarero, a
el tamaño
el regalo

SHOPPING

(caro, barato) el dólar
la receta el peso
la planta la planta baja,
la primera planta segunda planta
la tercera planta la peseta
la tarjeta de crédito los cheques de viajeros
el dinero en efectivo el euro
la panadería el pan
la heladería el helado
la carnicería la carne
la pastelería las tortas y los pasteles
el mercado la comida
el supermercado los comestibles
la zapataría los zapatos
la pescadería el pescado
la joyería las joyas
la librería los libros
la farmacia la medicina
el almacén   (Shops are also mentioned in communities and neighborhoods)

Las Actividades:

llevar ponerse
comprar vender
usar querer
ir poder
pagar probarse
costar quedarse

Las Expresiones:

¿Cuánto cuesta? ¿Dónde se prueba la ropa?
¿Cómo puedo pagar? ¿Aceptan Uds. tarjetas de créditos?
¿Qué talla usa Ud.? ¿Quieres ir de compras?
¿A qué hora? ¿En qué puedo servirle?
¿Qué prefieres? (No) me queda bien.
Lo siento. la ropa de moda

El euro

To find the number of euros equal to a certain number of pesetas, divide the number of pesetas by 166.386. for example: One pair of shoes that cost 7,650 pesetas costs 45.98 euros.

SHOPPING

Pre-Testing Activities

1. Divide the class into groups of three or four students. Give each group an index card on which is written a family member. Then give the students three minutes to write as many articles of clothing as they can for the family on their card. At the end of three minutes, review the answers of all the members orally. Award a prize (extra-credit, a sticker, or anything you feel is appropriate) to the group that has the most answers.

2. Divide the class again into groups of three or four students. Use the same procedure as above except write a season on the card.

3. Have students bring old ties, shirts, hats or any clothing that their parents will allow. Say what they are and who wears them. Then, have students play the role of the customer and salesclerk. *To make the purchase realistic, provide examples of Spanish or Hispanic currency and discuss the Euro.

4. Provide the class with authentic ads for sales from Spanish newspapers. Discuss sizes and currency and the Euro.

5. Have the class make a collage of the articles of clothing labeling them on the collage or an attached list. They may also make a booklet or brochure of clothing in which the articles are categorized by seasons.

6. Bring in a bag or suitcase full of items for the students to identify. Tell them your friend went shopping for you and you need help identifying the items and must know the kind of store where the item was bought. A list may be recorded on the chalkboard.

7. Have the students draw floor plans of a department store. Display the students' work in the classroom.

8. View taped commercials in Spanish with the students. Compare and contrast them with commercials in your country.

9. For extra credit, students bring to class product labels from home, which are printed in English and Spanish. These labels will form an on-going class bulletin board display.

SHOPPING

Useful Cultural Concepts For This Chapter

- Business hours
- Spanish fashion designers
- Spanish sizes
- The Spanish Euro or the Hispanic Peso

Los Refranes:

Lo barato sale caro.
La buena vida es cara. Hay otra, pero no es vida.

SCHOOL- TO- WORK

Show the class a video on Spanish fashion designers. For extra credit, have students bring to class magazine pictures of Spanish fashions and make a display on the school or class bulletin board. (Fashion videos may be purchased from the Spanish Cultural Services.)

SPEAKING SITUATIONS FOR PART 1 OF THE EXAM   (30%)

1. You are going shopping for a clothing gift for your best friend. You are going to his/her birthday party this evening. Greet the sales clerk and ask for suggestions. Tell him/her if you like the ideas he/she has given.

2. You are going to camp for two weeks. Convince your father that you   need certain clothing and other items.

3. Your mother is accompanying you to the store to buy school clothes.
    React unfavorably to the clothes she has chosen and suggest other clothing.

4.   You are at a dance with your friends. Socialize with them by discussing
    the clothes other people are wearing.

SHOPPING

TEACHER'S SCRIPT FOR THE EXAM, PART II (Listening, 30%)

Part 2a. Directions: For each question, you will hear some background information in English. Then you will hear a passage in Spanish twice, followed by the question in English. Listen carefully. After you have heard the question, read the question and the four suggested answers on your test paper. Choose the best answer and write its number in the appropriate space on your answer sheet.

1. María and Paula are talking about their plans for the weekend. Paula says:

   María, yo quiero ir al almacén este sábado porque yo necesito comprar un vestido elegante para un baile formal.

   Why is Paula going to the store? (3)

2. You are in a store and hear this announcement.

   Buenas tarde, Señoras y Señores. Hoy tenemos una ganga especial en el departamento de ropa para hombres: corbatas por $10.00, y pantalones por $25.00.

   What is on sale today? (2)

3. Marco goes into a shop at the mall and speaks to a salesperson.

   El empleado: ¿En que puedo servirle, señor?.
   Marco: Yo quiero comprar un regalo para mi madre.
   El empleado: ¿Qué desea Ud. comprar?
   Marco: Yo quisiera una blusa amarilla.
   El empleado: Muy bien. ¿Le gusta ésta?
   Marco: Sí, es perfecta.

   Why is Marco shopping? (4)

Part 2b Directions: For each question, you will hear some background information in English. Then you will hear a passage in Spanish twice, followed by the question in Spanish. Listen carefully. After you have heard the question, read the question and the four suggested answers on your test paper. Choose the best answer and write its number on your answer sheet.

4. Ramón is speaking with his grandmother. His grandmother says:

   Ramón yo necesito pan y leche de la tienda por favor. Toma diez dólares y ve al supermercado después de las clases hoy.

   ¿Qué hace Ramón para su abuela? (2)

5. You are ready to make a purchase at a department store. You are speaking to the salesperson.

   <u>Tú:</u> Perdón, señor, yo quiero comprar esta falda.
   <u>El empleado:</u> Muy bien, ¿Cómo va a pagar?
   <u>Tú:</u> ¿Aceptan Uds. tarjetas de crédito?
   <u>El empleado:</u> Lo siento. Solamente aceptamos cheques de
                              viajeros o dinero en efectivo.
   <u>Tú:</u> Bueno, yo tengo un cheque de viajeros.

   ¿Cómo vas a pagar la cuenta? (3)

6. Carmen and Susana are talking about their new jobs.

   Carmen dice, "Me gusta ser empleada en una tienda de ropa porque puedo
                  comprar ropa nueva con un descuento de 20%".
   Susana dice, "Sí, tienes razón. Es maravilloso. Ahora puedo tener la ropa de
                  moda en vez de la ropa de mi hermana mayor.

   ¿Por qué les gusta trabajar en una tienda a las chicas? (4)

Part 2c Directions: For each question, you will hear some background information in English. Then you will hear a passage in Spanish twice, followed by the question in English. Listen carefully. After you have heard the question, read the question and look at the four pictures in your test. Choose the picture that best answers the question and write its number in the appropriate space on your answer sheet. (12%)

7. Mrs. Gómez is shopping with her daughter. Her daughter says:

   Mamá necesito una blusa nueva porque voy a un baile esta noche en mi colegio. Me gusta esta blusa bonita con las flores. El color azul es mi favorito.

   What does the girl want to buy? (3)

SHOPPING

8. Mr. González is doing errands. He says to the clerk

Buenos días, señor. Yo quiero comprar el arroz, los plátanos y las legumbres. A mi familia no le gusta comer en los restaurantes porque yo soy cocinero.

Where is he? (1)

9. José and his mother are talking about what he should wear. He says:

- Quiero trabajar para esta compañía importante. Y quiero llevar la ropa apropiada. ¿Debo llevar esta corbata nueva con este traje negro y camisa blanca?
- Sí, José, esa ropa es muy distinguida.

What items if clothing will he be wearing? (3)

10. Pancho is talking with his friend Héctor.

¿Has escuchado el nuevo disco compacto de Gloria Estefan? Es fantástico y muy animado. Yo quiero ir a la tienda para comprarlo. ¿Quieres ir conmigo?

What does Pancho want to buy? (2)

Reading Comprehension answers:

3a. (8%)	11. 2	12. 2	13. 1	14. 1
3b. (12%)	15. 3	16. 1	17. 3	18. 4

SHOPPING

EXAMINATION

Part 1.   **Speaking** (30%)
Part 2.   **Listening** (30%)

Part 2 a. Directions: For each question, you will hear some background information in English. Then you will hear a passage in Spanish twice, followed by the question in English. Listen carefully. After you have heard the question, read the question and the four suggested answers on your test paper. Choose the best answer and write its number in the appropriate space on your answer sheet.

1. Why is Paula going to this store?
   1. She needs food for a dinner party
   2. She needs furniture for her house.
   3. She needs a new dress for a dance.
   4. She needs clothing for a trip.

2. What is on sale today?
   1. ties and pants
   2. pants and sweaters
   3. shoes and ties
   4. socks and shoes

3. Why is Marco shopping?
   1. He needs a lamp for his room.
   2. He needs a book to read.
   3. He needs a stamp for his collection.
   4. He needs a present for his mother.

Part 2 b. Directions: For each question, you will hear some background information in English. Then you will hear a passage in Spanish twice, followed by the question in Spanish. Listen carefully. After you have heard the question, read the question and the four suggested answers on your test paper. Choose the best answer and write its number in the appropriate space on your answer sheet.

4. ¿Qué hace Ramón para su abuela?
   1. El va a lavar los platos.
   2. El va a comprar comida para ella.
   3. El va a la carnicería.
   4. El va al banco.

5. ¿Cómo vas a pagar la cuenta?
   1. con dinero en efectivo
   2. con tarjetas de crédito
   3. con cheques de viajeros
   4. con un cheque personal

6. ¿Por qué les gusta trabajar en una tienda a las chicas?
   1. La tienda está cerca de su casa.
   2. Reciben mucho dinero.
   3. Hablan con sus amigos.
   4. Compran ropa en la tienda.

SHOPPING

Part 2c Directions: For each question, you will hear some background information in English. Then you will hear a passage in Spanish twice, followed by the question in English. Listen carefully. After you have heard the question, read the question and look at the four pictures in your test. Choose the picture that best answers the question and write the appropriate answer on your answer sheet.

7. What does the girl want to buy?

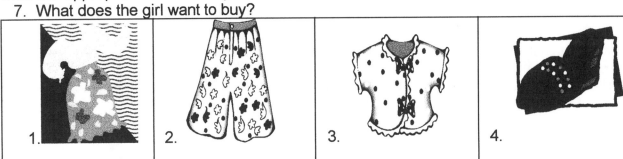

8. Where is he?

9. What items of clothing will he be wearing?

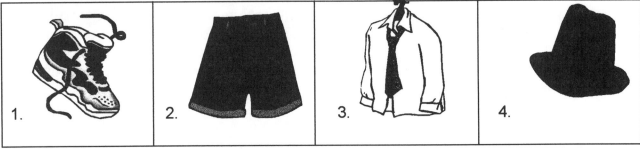

10. What does Pancho want to buy?

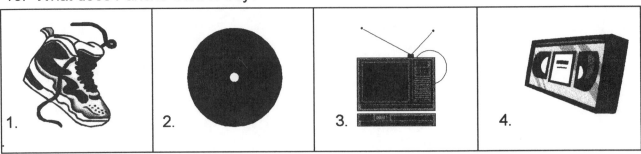

Part 3: READING (20%) Directions: Answer the questions in English based on the reading selection in Spanish. Choose the best answer to each question. Base your choice on the content of the reading selection. Write the number of your best answer in the appropriate space on your answer sheet.

11. According to this ad, what time does the store close on Saturdays?

    1. eight   3. five
    2. nine   4. three

Baratísimo r Us

EL CENTRO COMERCIAL PARA TODA LA FAMILIA

http://www.barato.com

¡Sorteo Gratís!   ¡Sorteo Gratís!

1er premio: UNA GRABADORA DE VIDEO CASSETTE

TAMBIÉN LES RECORDAMOS QUE CONTINUAMOS CON LOS DESCUENTOS
DEL 30% AL 60%

ESTA OFERTA EN TODAS NUESTRAS SELECCIONES:

ROPA DE NIÑOS Y SEÑORAS   ZAPATOS, PARA SEÑORAS Y NIÑOS
ALQUILER- ROPA DE ETIQUETA   ROPA DE MUJER
SALÓN DE BELLEZA   TIENDA DE BLUE JEANS
PERFUMERÍA Y COSMÉTICOS   ELECTRO DOMÉSTICOS
JOYERÍA   LIBRERÍA

Desde las 10 - las 22

VENGA Y COMPRE.........
......EN UN AMBIENTE AGRADABLE Y CÓMODO.   GRACIAS

(EL SORTEO SE CELEBRARÁ EL 12 DE NOVIEMBRE DE 2004)

12.   What would you be able to buy at this center?
   1. dinner   2. bicycles
   3. jewelry   4. cars

13.   Why should you shop there?
   1. There is a comfortable, agreeable atmosphere.
   2. It is near the train.
   3. They have a contest every day.
   4. They are open 24 hours.

14.   Why would you buy clothing there?
   1. The store has up to a 60% discount.
   2. They have designer dresses.
   3. There is a sale on Sunday.
   4. They refund your money after 3 weeks.

Part 3b Directions: Answer the Spanish questions based on the reading selection in Spanish. Choose the best answer to each question. Write the number of your answer in the appropriate space on your answer sheet.

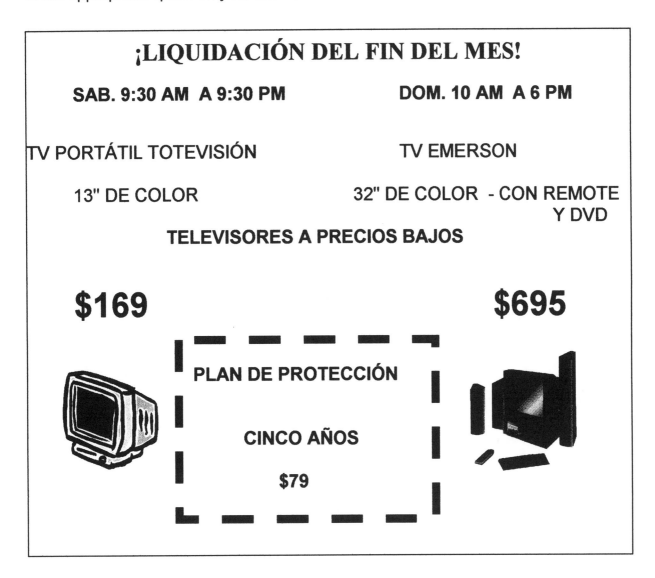

15. ¿Por qué se compran televisores aquí?
    1. Los televisores cuestan $50.00.
    2. Hay buenos vendedores.
    3. Hay un buen plan de servicios.
    4. Hay refrigeradores y estufas.

16. El televisor más barato cuesta…
    1. $169   3. $79
    2. $695   4. $179

ECONOMICE HASTA EL 70%

Ropa para Caballeros, de diseñadores famosos

TRAJES   2 TRAJES POR $200

CHAQUETAS   3 CHAQUETAS POR $130
DEPORTIVAS

PANTALONES DE VESTIR   2 POR $50
CAMISAS DE VESTIR   2 POR $40

ABIERTO LOS SIETE DÍAS

17. ¿Qué se vende en esta tienda?

     1. ropa para damas.
     2. ropa para niños.
     3. ropa para hombres.
     4. ropa para la familia.

18. Tú necesitas dos trajes y dos pantalones de vestir.
     ¿Cuánto cuestan en total?

     1. $200   3. $400
     2. $150   4. $250

PART 4: WRITING (20%)

Part 4a. Directions: Choose two of the three writing tasks provided below. Your answer to each of the two questions should be written entirely in Spanish and should contain a minimum of **20 words**.

Place names and brand names written in Spanish count as one word. Contractions are counted as one word. Salutations, closing, and commonly used abbreviations are included in the word count. Numbers, unless written as words, and names of people do not count as words.

Be sure that you have satisfied the purpose of the task. The sentence structure and/or expressions used should be connected logically and demonstrate a wide range of vocabulary with minimal repetition.

4a. You have just celebrated your birthday and have received many new clothes. Write a note of twenty words in Spanish to your best friend describing the gifts and tell why you like them. You may wish to include:

- The items you received
- The color and size
- The reason you like them
- The person who gave them to you
- What you will do with the gifts

4b. Write a message in Spanish to your roommate telling him or her that you needed to go to the store to buy some items for a picnic that you are planning. You may wish to include:

- The name(s) and description(s) of the place(s) you are going to
- Whom you are going with
- Why you are going there
- When you are going there
- The items you needed to buy

4c. You are an exchange student in Cuernavaca, Mexico. Monday is the first day of school. Of course, you must go shopping because you need many new things for school. Write a note in Spanish to your mother telling her that you must go shopping and the items that you need. You may wish to include:

- The types of items you need to buy
- Where the items are available
- When you will be going
- With whom you will be going
- How much money you need to spend
- Ask if you can use her credit card

SHOPPING

ANSWER SHEET

Nombre_____ **Fecha**_____

PART 1: SPEAKING (30%) _____
PART 2: LISTENING (30%)   **PART 3: READING** (20%)

2a.	2b.	2c.	3a.(8%)	3b.(12%)
1._____	4._____	7._____	11._____	15._____
2._____	5._____	8._____	12._____	16._____
3._____	6._____	9._____	13._____	17._____
		10._____	14._____	18._____

PART 4: WRITING (20%) **20 WORDS   4a , 4b or 4c Write 2 paragraphs**

1_____

_____

_____

_____

_____

_____

_____

_____

_____

2_____

_____

_____

_____

_____

_____

_____

_____

_____

SHOPPING

Authentic Assestment

Winning a shopping spree

Situation: ¡Felicidades! You have just won the International Shopping Spree Contest. As the grand prize winner, you will receive an all expense paid trip to any city in the Spanish speaking world. Upon arrival, you will be allowed to shop for one hour or spend 1.000.000 euros/pesos, whichever occurs first. Anything you select is yours to keep, free of charge. You may buy only one of each item you select.

1. Research what famous products are produced in the country you have chosen and the names of at least two well-known stores located there.

2. *¡Organiza*! Organize your shopping by completing the columns below so that you do not miss out on anything you would like purchase.

PRODUCTOS	DESCRIPCIONES	TIENDAS	PRECIOS

3. You are unsure if a certain store sells an item you would like to purchase. Put a message on the store's answering machine inquiring if the product is sold there. Ask about the price and any other pertinent information. Tell how and when you can be reached. You will use and audio tape to record your message.

4. The big shopping day has been a great success. You have just returned to your hotel after a gala celebration dinner in your honor. You are too excited to sleep. Include how you feel about this experience.

Health and Welfare

HEALTH AND WELFARE

Las Partes del Cuerpo:

la boca
el brazo
el cabello
la cabeza
la cara
el cuello
los dedos
el diente
el estómago
la frente
la garganta
el hombre
el hombro
la lengua
la mano
la mujer
la nariz
el oído
el ojo
la oreja
el pecho
el pelo
el pie
la piel
la pierna
la rodilla

Las Actividades:

comer
correr
hablar
oír
oler
pensar
tocar

La Salud:

la aspirina
el brazo roto
el enfermero,a
la epidemia

la farmacia
la fiebre
la gripe
el hospital
la indigestión
la jarabe (para la tos)
la medicina
el médico,a
el paciente
la pierna rota
la píldora
la receta
el resfriado (tener)
la rubeola
el sarampión
el SIDA
el seguro médico
la varicela
la viruela
la vitamina

Los Adjetivos:

enfermo,a
débil
delicado
estar bien/mal
grave
mareado,a

Las Actividades:

estar + physical conditions
doler (me duele)
mejorar
necesitar
ponerse mal
recetar
recomendar
tener dolor de _____ (body part)
tener + illness or condition
tomar (medicina, aspirina)

HEALTH AND WELFARE

Las Expresiones:

¿Qué tiene(s)?
Yo tengo_____. (illness or condition)
¿Cómo está(s)?
Estoy _____
No me siento bien
¿Qué te (le) duele?

Me duele_____
¡Es lástima!
¡Ojalá que_____!
Es necesario que_____
Es importante que_____
Es posible que_____
Recomiendo que_____
Vaya a _____
Quiero que _____

PRE-TESTING ACTIVITIES

1. After teaching the body parts, the teacher can lead the class in Simon Says. The next day the students may try to do the same.

2. Students may make an original drawing or model of a robot and label the body parts. A prize can be given for the best one.

3. The teacher asks for volunteers to go the board. The students at their seats may work in their notebooks or on a piece of paper given out by the teacher. The teacher dictates the description of a person or just a face. The students must draw what they hear as accurately as possible.

4. The students sit in paired groups and pretend to be doctor and patient. The doctor asks in Spanish, ¿Qué tienes? The patient answers appropriately. The students then reverse roles.

5. The teacher distributes a form for admission to the emergency room (*La Sala de Urgencias*). The students sit in pairs, one playing the role of receptionist, the other of the patient. (This will review the material learned in the topic of Personal identification as well as reinforce what is learned in Health and Welfare) They may even then reverse roles.

6. In Spanish, students tell in what ways their parents can improve the health of their children.

USEFUL CULTURAL CONCEPTS FOR THIS CHAPTER

- U.S. drugstore vs. la farmacia
- El curandero
- El boticario
- Carlos J. Finlay M.D. and William Gorgas M.D.

HEALTH AND WELFARE

Los Refranes:
- El ejercicio le hace maestro.
- A caballo regalado, no le mires el diente.
- Cuesta un ojo de la cara.
- En boca cerrada no entran moscas.
- Cada cabeza es un mundo.
- Sana, sana, colita de rana, si no sanas hoy sanarás mañana.

SCHOOL-TO-WORK

Role-play showing how Spanish could be of help with a patient in a local doctor's office or hospital.

SPEAKING SITUATIONS FOR PART 1 OF THE EXAM (30%)

1. You had an accident on your bicycle last week. You have a broken arm. You are returning to the doctor for a check-up. Greet the doctor and tell him/her how you are feeling.

2. You are at your grandparent's house. He/She hasn't been feeling well for a week. Greet him/her and ask about his/her health. Give your reaction to his/her responses.

3. You are on vacation and feel ill. Go to the pharmacy and tell the pharmacist about your symptoms. Convince him/her to recommend some medicine.

4. Your classmate is ill. Telephone him/her to inquire about his/her health.

TEACHER'S SCRIPT FOR THE EXAM, PART II (Listening, 30%)

Part 2a. Directions: For each question, you will hear some background information in English. Then you will hear a passage in Spanish twice, followed by the question in English. Listen carefully. After you have heard the question, read the question and the four suggested answers on your test paper. Choose the best answer and write its number in the appropriate space on your answer sheet.

1. You and Juan are talking about an accident happening right now. He says:

    Mira ese auto. Va muy rápidamente. El chico cruza la calle sin mirar. ¡Qué accidente! El pobre chico. Probablemente él tiene un brazo roto.

    What happened to the person crossing the street? (2)

HEALTH AND WELFARE

2. Emilio is listening to his favorite radio station and hears this commercial.

¿Es el color de los dientes un problema para Ud.? ¿Están muy amarillos a causa de fumar o de beber té o café? Resuelva su problema con la mejor pasta dental. Cepíllese los dientes con "Blanquísimo".

What does this commercial suggest you do? (4)

3. Margarita is talking to the doctor. She says:

Doctor Pineda, yo tengo un dolor del oído. También me duele la garganta. ¿Qué recomienda Ud.?

What is one of the girl's complaints? (1)

Part 2b. Directions: For each question, you will hear some background information in English. Then you will hear a passage in Spanish twice, followed by the question in Spanish. Listen carefully. After you have heard the question, read the question and the four suggested answers on your test paper. Choose the best answer and write its number in the appropriate space on your answer sheet.

4. Your aunt is calling her son's elementary school. She says:

¡Hola! Soy la madre de Pepito Morales. Él no asiste a las clases hoy porque tiene fiebre y está mareado. Muchas gracias. Adiós.

¿Qué problema tiene Pepito? (3)

5. You are watching TV and you hear this public service announcement.

Atención padres de todos los niños entre las edades de seis años y doce años. Sus niños necesitan inyecciones contra la varicela este año. Hay la posibilidad de una epidemia.

¿Por qué necesitan los niños una inyección? (1)

6. You are shopping and hear a customer asking for help. The clerk greets him and says

-¿En qué puedo servirle, señor?
-Yo necesito medicina para la indigestión.

-Muy bien. Puedo recomendar ésta.
-Muchas gracias, muy amable.

¿Dónde está el hombre? (4)

Part 2c. Directions: For each question, you will hear some background information in English. Then you will hear a passage in Spanish twice, followed by the question in Spanish. Listen carefully. After you have heard the question, read the question and look at the four pictures on your test paper. Choose the picture that best answers the question and write its number in the appropriate space on your answer sheet.

7.   A man comes into the emergency room and says:

        ¡Ayúdeme por favor! Yo tuve un accidente con mi bicicleta. Creo que tengo la nariz rota.

        Which picture shows what happened to the man? (1)

8.   You hear this interview on the radio.

        Me llamo Tomás García. Yo juego el fútbol con los Piratas de Lima, Perú. No estoy jugando ahora porque yo tengo la pierna rota. ¡Ojalá que yo regrese el año que viene!

        What item(s) will Tomás García need? (2)

9.   Carlos is ill. He goes to the hospital where he speaks to a doctor. He says:

        -Buenos días, Dr. Menéndez. No me siento bien hoy. Me duele el estómago, estoy mareado y tengo fiebre. ¿Qué me recomienda?
        -Bueno, Carlos, es la viruela. Toma dos píldoras cada 4 horas. Llámame mañana.

        What does Carlos need? (2)

10.   Two people are discussing a photo. One says:

Ella es muy bonita. Tiene el pelo rubio y largo, los ojos azules, la boca pequeña y los dientes blancos. Ella va a ganar el primer premio en el concurso de belleza, La Señorita Sudaméricana.

Who is being described? (4)

Reading Comprehension answers:

3a (8%)	11.3	12.4	13.4	14.1
3b (12%)	15.2	16.3	17.2	18.3

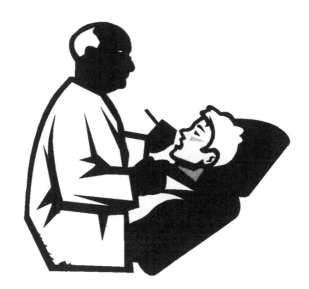

HEALTH AND WELFARE

Nombre_____ Fecha_____

EXAMINATION

PART I. SPEAKING (30%)
PART 2. LISTENING (30%)

Part 2a. Directions: For each question, you will hear some background information in English. Then you will hear a passage in Spanish twice, followed by the question in English. Listen carefully. After you have heard the question, read the question and the four suggested answers on your test paper. Choose the best answer and write its number in the appropriate space on your answer sheet.

1 What happened to the person crossing the street?
   1. He got in a cab.   3. He was hit by a bicycle.
   2. He was hit by a car.   4. He was hit by a bus.

2. What does this commercial suggest you do?
   1. use deodorant   3. buy dandruff shampoo
   2. use mouthwash   4. buy toothpaste

3. What is one of the girl's complaints?
   1. a sore throat   3. a headache
   2. back pain   4. nausea

Part 2b. Directions: For each question, you will hear some background information in English. Then you will hear a passage in Spanish twice, followed by the question in Spanish. Listen carefully. After you have heard the question, read the question and the four suggested answers on your test paper. Choose the best answer and write its number in the appropriate space on your answer sheet.

4. ¿Qué problema tiene Pepito?
   1. Él está sucio.   3. Él está enfermo.
   2. Él tiene miedo.   4. Él durmió tarde.

5. ¿Por qué necestian los niños una inyección?
   1. Porque no quieren una epidemia.
   2. No tienen seguro médico.
   3. Vienen de otro país.
   4. Hay muchos casos de gripe.

6. ¿Dónde está el hombre?
   1. En la tienda de ropa   3. En el supermercado
   2. En el correo   4. En la farmacia

HEALTH AND WELFARE

Part 2c. Directions: For each question, you will hear some background information in English. Then you will hear a passage in Spanish twice, followed by the question in Spanish. Listen carefully. After you have heard the question, read the question and look at the four pictures on your test paper. Choose the picture that best answers the question and write its number in the appropriate space on your answer sheet.

7.   Which picture shows what happened to the man?

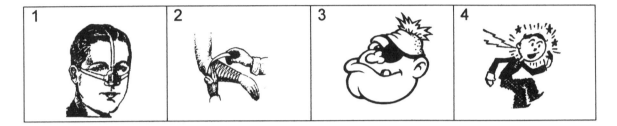

8. What item(s) will Tomás García use?

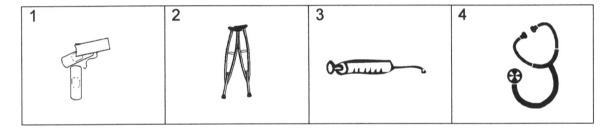

9. What does Carlos need?

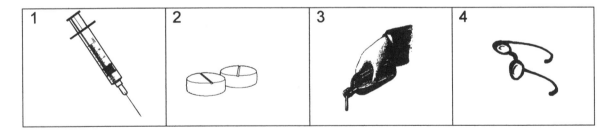

10. Who is being described?

Part 3a. Directions: Answer the questions in English based on the reading selections in Spanish. Choose the best answer to each question. Base your choice on the content of the reading selection. Write the number of your answer in the appropriate space on your answer sheet.

MEDICOS

1 157 **Psiquiatras**	3 159 **Dermatólogos**
Dr. César Jardín **Psiquiatra** Interés especial en pacientes difíciles de mejorar. Consultorio en Manhattan Llame (212) 555-0954	**Dra. Pilar Brand** *Certificada por la Junta Americana de Dermotología* ♦ Dermotología de niños ♦ Desórdenes de la piel, cabello y uñas 500 E. Calle 39 (212) 555-6543
2 156 **Alergías**	4 160 **Podiatría**
Dr. Pedro Gonzálvez *Asma/Alergía/Pediatría* ¿Síntomas de resfriado todo el año? Llame (718) 555-3456 92-56 Avenida Kissena	**Dr. Jesús Fisher** ¿Dolor de pies? *Especialista de los pies* Se habla español Teléfono: (718) 555-2378

11. If you have skin problems, whom would you call?

    1 (1)   2. (2)   3. (3)   4. (4)

12. If you have pain and cannot walk, whom will you call?

    1 (1)   2. (2)   3. (3)   4. (4)

Sin alcohol

Este producto de Marchy con propiedades bactericidas, puede ser una solución muy apropiada para quienes tienen un problema de sudor excesivo y una piel delicada y sensible. (1510 Pesetas) (9,06euros)

13. What is this ad selling?
   - 1. hand lotion
   - 2. powder
   - 3. make-up
   - 4. deodorant

14. According to this ad, who should buy this product?
   - 1. people with sensitive skin
   - 2. people with sensitive eyes
   - 3. people with sunburn
   - 4. people with acne

Part 3b. Directions: Answer the question based on the reading selection in Spanish. Choose the best answer to each question and write the number in the appropriate space on your answer sheet.

Mejórate físicamente

Con nuestros prácticos y utilísimos aparatos podrás MONTAR TU GIMNASIO en tu propia casa.

Y utilizándolos solo diez minutos diarios, podrás convertirte un un ATLETA admirado.

Puedes desarrollar los músculos de la mano, hombro, y también los músculos de las piernas
Centro De la Hoya, Calle Montoya, 627 Caracas

15. Según este anuncio, ¿qué mejorará?
   - 1. el pelo
   - 2. el cuerpo
   - 3. los pies
   - 4. la cara

16. ¿Por cuánto tiempo es necesario usar este aparato?
   - 1. un día
   - 2. tres días por semana
   - 3. menos de quince minutos cada día
   - 4. cinco horas por día

EL AGUA PURA

Proteja su salud tomando agua limpia y cristalina sin sabor ni olor al cloro y sin sedimentos.

¿Y Cómo?

Con Alardo y Gómez

El Filtro #1
No acepte imitaciones

Llame 63-42-31
$170 Modelo 438

---

17. ¿Qué se vende, según este anuncio?
    1. una secadora
    2. un sistema de purificación de agua
    3. una estufa
    4. un sistema para aire acondicionado

18. Este sistema limpia...
    1. el aire
    2. las alfombras
    3. el agua
    4. los platos

PART 4 WRITING (20%)

Part 4 Directions: Choose two of the three writing tasks provided below. Your answer to each of the two questions should be written entirely in Spanish and should contain a minimum of **30 words**.

Place names and brand names written in Spanish count as one word. Contractions are counted as one word. Salutations, closing, and commonly used abbreviations are included in the word count. Numbers, unless written as words, and names of people do not count as words.

Be sure that you have satisfied the purpose of the task. The sentence structure and/or expressions used should be connected logically and demonstrate a wide range of vocabulary with minimal repetition.

HEALTH AND WELFARE

4a. You have been invited to spend the week at your aunt's summer home in Málaga, Spain. Unfortunately you have become ill. Write a note in Spanish telling her why you cannot come for a visit. You may wish to include:

- The date of the visit
- The reason you can't visit.
- Your symptoms
- An expression of your regret and sorrow.
- A suggestion of another day for your visit.

4b. Your friend from Venezuela is thinking of having plastic surgery. Write a note to your friend in which, you mention a part of your body that you would like to change and tell why. You may wish to include:

- The item you would like to change
- The reason you would like to change it.
- The benefits you will have from the change
- The opinion of your parents
- The opinion of your friends

4c. Your favorite magazine is asking for ways that you think are safe to lose weight. Write a note to Lulu, the writer of the health column, in which you give your opinion and ideas for weight loss. You may wish to include:

- Ideas for the types of meals to make
- Ideas for the food to buy
- Ideas for physical activity
- Ideas about consulting a doctor
- The reasons that being over weight or under weight are not healthy

HEALTH AND WELFARE

ANSWER SHEET

Nombre_____ **Fecha**_____

PART 1: SPEAKING (30%) _____
PART 2: LISTENING (30%)   **PART 3: READING** (20%)

2a.	2b.	2c.		3a.(8%)	3b.(12%)
1._____	4._____	7._____		11._____	15._____
2._____	5._____	8._____		12._____	16._____
3._____	6._____	9._____		13._____	17._____
		10._____		14._____	18._____

PART 4: WRITING (20%) **30 WORDS   4a , 4b or 4c Write 2 paragraphs**

1_____

_____

_____

_____

_____

_____

_____

_____

_____

2_____

_____

_____

_____

_____

_____

_____

_____

_____

_____

HEALTH AND WELFARE

AUTHENTIC ASSESSMENT
Helping a doctor

Situation: Your friend's older sister, Diana, is a doctor who will leave shortly for Guatemala as a volunteer for *Médicos sin Fronteras*. Since you are studying Spanish, Diana asks for your help in preparation for her new duties.

1. Prepare a booklet for Diana in which you draw or use pictures of body parts and organs labeled in Spanish. Diana will use this booklet as a communication aid with her patients. Also write out for her the Spanish names of at least 10 different illnesses, injuries or medical conditions. Finally, make a list in Spanish of at least 10 recommendations Diana might make to a patient.

2. To assist Diana with her patients, role-play with her in a doctor/patient interview and consultation in Spanish. One of your classmates can play the role of Diana, while you play the role of the patient.

PHYSICAL
ENVIRONMENT

Las Estaciones del Año:
el invierno
la primavera
el otoño
el verano

Los Meses:
enero
febrero
marzo
abril
mayo
junio
julio
agosto
septiembre
octubre
noviembre
diciembre

El Clima y El Tiempo:
buen tiempo
la bola de nieve
el calor
el cielo
el clima
el frío
la humedad
la lluvia
el mal tiempo
la nieve
el pronóstico
el sol
el tiempo
el viento

Las Actividades:
acampar
correr
escalar montañas
esquiar
ir al cine
jugar los deportes
nadar
pescar

tomar el sol

Las Expresiones:
¿Qué tiempo hace?
Hace frío
calor
sol
viento
fresco
buen tiempo
mal tiempo
¿Cómo estás?
Tengo frío
calor
¿Qué haces en (season)?
¿Qué haces cuando (type of weather)?
Nevar (nieva)
Llover (llueve)
Está nublado
Bajo cero
Vientos leves
Alrededor de ____°
Farenheit
Centígrado
To change Fahrenheit to Centigrade
$$\frac{(°F - 32) \times 5}{9} = °C$$
To change Centigrade to Farenheit
$$\frac{(°C \times 9)}{5} + 32 = °F$$

El Mapa y La Geografía:
el árbol
los animales
las avenidas
el barrio
el bosque
los bulevares
la calle
el campo
la ciudad
el desierto
el edificio
el este

PHYSICAL ENVIRONMENT

el campo
la ciudad
el desierto
el edificio
el este
la granja
la isla
al lago
el mar
las montañas
el norte
el océano
el oeste
las plantas
la playa
el pueblo
el rascacielos
el río
el sur
el tránsito
el vecino (a)
el vecindario

Las Actividades

estar
ir a
preferir
quedar
ver
visitar
vivir

Las Expresiones:

¿Dónde está_____?
Está cerca de/lejos de_____
¿Dónde vive(s)?
Vivo en_____
¿Qué hay en tu pueblo/ciudad?
¿Qué haces en_____?
¿Cómo es_____?
Es enorme (hermoso, pequeño)

PRE-TESTING ACTIVITIES:

1. Divide the class into four groups by counting off. Give the students an index card with a season of the year written in English. The students must write the season in Spanish and then list all the months that belong in that season. Finally, they must write two activities in which they engage at that time of the year.

2. Show four or more pictures of different seasons and activities taking place at that time of the year on an overhead transparency projector or mounted on oaktag. Describe the pictures. The students must match the description with the picture.

3. Tape the weather report in Spanish on a cassette tape or on videotape. Photocopy comprehension questions based on the tape. Students answer the questions based on the report(s) they hear.

4. Divide the class into four groups. Assign each group to a season. Each group must make up a weather report and add activities that are appropriate for the weather. Groups may illustrate the weather and activities

5. At the beginning of class, have the students sit with their conversation partners and greet one another. Then they should talk about the weather, their neighborhood and what they do there.

6. The teacher places a blank transparency on the overhead projector. Then he/she should ask the class, *¿Qué hay en el campo?* As the students give the description, the teacher will draw the things mentioned in Spanish on the transparency to create a funny and poorly drawn country scene.

7. The same procedure may be used (as in #6) to review and reinforce the vocabulary for the city. As a homework assignment, the students should draw and label their own versions of the city and country. These will be used the next day in paired groups in which the students can describe their pictures, ask questions about their partner's drawings or decide which they prefer more, the city or the country.

8. The teacher can show a map of Spain on an overhead projector. The bordering countries can be reviewed or the geography of Spain can be discussed pointing at major rivers, mountains, surrounding bodies of water, etc. At this time the teacher can introduce: norte, sur, este, oeste. Then the students can be assigned to make their own maps of Spain or other Spanish-speaking countries, labeling the geographical features. (Refer to the maps)

9. Two students may be sent to the board to draw what the teacher or another student dictates. The class will draw in their notebooks. A country or city scene can be dictated.

USEFUL CULTURAL CONCEPTS FOR THIS CHAPTER

*   Discussion of the Fahrenheit and Celsius formulas
*   A library unit on the various aspects of Spain or other Spanish-speaking countries
*   A map study of Spain including major geographical features, most important cities and borders

Los Refranes:

*   La primavera la sangre altera.
*   Él que planta árboles ama a otros además de a sí mismo.
*   Quien va a Sevilla, pierde su silla.
*   Llueve a cántaros.
*   A mal tiempo, buena cara
*   Abril, aguas mil
*   Año de nieves, año de bienes
*   Marzo ventoso y abril lluvioso hacen a mayo florido y hermoso.

PHYSICAL ENVIRONMENT

SCHOOL-TO-WORK

Students briefly research the following professions and write one example of how knowing Spanish could be of use in each profession: archeologist, architect, astronaut, astronomer, botanist, environmental disaster specialist, geologist, marine biologist, mining engineer, ornithologist and ship captain. Students share their examples in class.

SPEAKING SITUATIONS FOR PART I OF THE EXAM (30%)

1. You and your friend are planning a vacation. You are discussing the season in which you would like to travel, the destination (city or country), the activities in which you would like to engage, and the climate.

2. You are going to visit a national park in Costa Rica. Request information from the guide as to the activities and the facilities available in the park.

3. You are staying at your cousin's house at the seashore. It's time to leave. Try to convince you parents by phone to let you stay by giving a description of the area and by telling what you are doing there.

4. Your parents are planning a trip to a large city. React favorably to this and suggest things to do in the city.

TEACHER'S SCRIPT FOR THE EXAM, PART II (Listening, 30%)

Part 2a. Directions: For each question, you will hear some background information in English. Then you will hear a passage in Spanish twice, followed by the question in English. Listen carefully. After you have heard the question, read the question and the four suggested answers on your test paper. Choose the best answer and write its number in the appropriate space on your answer sheet.

1. Rosamaría is talking with her family in the living room. She says:

    Me gusta esta estación del año mucho. Aquí en los Estados Unidos hace frío en diciembre cuando celebramos la Navidad.

    What holiday are they celebrating? (4)

PHYSICAL ENVIRONMENT

2.   The Ramírez family is on vacation. Mr. Ramírez says:

Me encanta viajar mucho pero el clima en Madrid en verano es malo.
Hace mucho calor. La temperatura es 94° Fahrenheit.

What is the weather like? (2)

3.   Luis hears this weather report on the radio.

Hay la posibilidad de lluvia esta noche. Va a llover desde las ocho de la
noche hasta las seis de la mañana. Viajar en carro o autobús será difícil.

What kind of weather is expected? (1)

Part 2b. Directions: For each question, you will hear some background
information in English. Then you will hear a passage in Spanish twice, followed
by the question in Spanish. Listen carefully. After you have heard the question,
read the question and the four suggested answers on your test paper. Choose
the best answer and write its number in the appropriate space on your answer
sheet.

4.   Ana is describing her father's occupation. She says:

Mi papá es policía. Él camina por las calles en mi barrio. Su ocupación es
difícil porque él trabaja cuando nieva o llueve. Hay muchos rascacielos
altos y mucho tráfico.

¿Dónde trabaja el padre de Ana? (2)

5.   You are talking with your friend Paula. She says:

¿Qué estación del año prefieres más? A mí me gusta esquiar en las
montañas y patinar sobre el hielo en el lago. Prefiero los deportes del
invierno.

¿Dónde debe pasar las vacaciones la chica? (1)

6.   Roberto's mother is talking to him before school. She says:

Roberto, hace mucho frío hoy. La temperatura está bajo cero. No camines
al colegio hoy. Toma el autobús.

¿Qué tiempo hace hoy? (4)

TEACHER'S SCRIPT FOR THE EXAM, PART II (Listening, 30%) (continued)

Part 2c. Directions: For each question, you will hear some background information in English. Then you will hear a passage in Spanish twice, followed by the question in Spanish. Listen carefully. After you have heard the question, read the question and look at the four pictures on your test paper. Choose the picture that best answers the question and write its number in the appropriate space on your answer sheet.

7. Mariluz is describing where she lives to her cousin who lives in Mexico. She says:

    Yo vivo en las montañas. Nieva mucho y yo juego con mis amigos en la nieve. Nos gusta tirar bolas de nieve y esquiar.

    Which picture shows where Mariluz lives? (2)

8. A travel agent is describing a vacation spot to you, He says:

    Se llama "El Lago Azul". Está en el bosque. El agua es clara y limpia. Puede pescar todo el día. También puede escalar montañas y acampar.

    Which vacation is he describing? (1)

9. Paco is telling his friends what he likes to do. He says:

    Durante el verano me gusta ir a la playa y nadar. Por la tarde yo escucho la radio y tomo el sol.

    What does he like to do? (3)

10. Rafael hears this weather forecast on the radio.

    Hoy hace viento y hace sol. Pero también hace fresco. La temperatura está a 57 grados. Es normal para esta estación del año. Lleve una chaqueta hoy.

    Which picture best shows the weather forecast? (4)

Reading Comprehension Answers:

3a (8%)	11.3	12.3	13.4	14.4
3b (12%)	15.2	16.3	17.1	18.1

PHYSICAL ENVIRONMENT

Nombre_____ Fecha_____

PART I. SPEAKING (30%)
PART 2. LISTENING (30%)

2a. Directions: For each question, you will hear some background information in English. Then you will hear a passage in Spanish twice, followed by the question in English. Listen carefully. After you have heard the question, read the question and the four suggested answers on your test paper. Choose the best answer and write its number in the appropriate space on your answer sheet.

1. What holiday are they celebrating?
    1. Easter
    2. Passover
    3. Thanksgiving
    4. Christmas

2. What is the weather like?
    1. It is cloudy.
    2. It is hot.
    3. It is snowing.
    4. It is raining.

3. What kind of weather is expected?
    1. a storm
    2. snow
    3. sun
    4. strong winds

2b. Directions: For each question, you will hear some background information in English. Then you will hear a passage in Spanish twice, followed by the question in Spanish. Listen carefully. After you have heard the question, read the question and the four suggested answers on your test paper. Choose the best answer and write its number in the appropriate space on your answer sheet.

4. ¿Dónde trabaja el padre de Ana?
    1. en la playa
    2. en la ciudad
    3. en las montañas
    4. en el campo

5. ¿Dónde debe pasar las vacaciones la chica?
    1. en los Andes
    2. en Florida
    3. en Acapulco
    4. en Puerto Rico

6. ¿Qué tiempo hace hoy?
    1. Hace viento.
    2. Hace sol.
    3. Hace calor.
    4. Hace frío.

PHYSICAL ENVIRONMENT

Part 2c. Directions: For each question, you will hear some background information in English. Then you will hear a passage in Spanish twice, followed by the question in Spanish. Listen carefully. After you have heard the question, read the question and look at the four pictures on your test paper. Choose the picture that best answers the question and write its number in the appropriate space on your answer sheet.

7. Which picture shows where Mariluz lives?

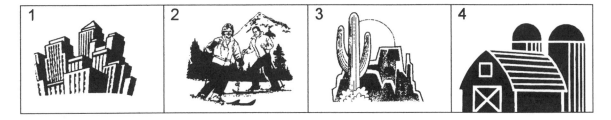

8. Which vacation is he describing?

9. What does he like to do?

10. Which picture best shows the weather forecast?

Part 3a. Directions: Answer the questions in English based on the reading selections in Spanish. Choose the best answer to each question. Base your choice on the content of the reading selections. Write the number of your answer in the appropriate space on your answer sheet.

El Tiempo

Temperatura mínima
24º a las 7:10

Presión: 1.007,9 milibares
Humedad: 64%
Cielo: nublado
Vientos: sector Noreste a 20 kmp/h

Pronóstico
En Santiago, Chile

Para hoy: caluroso y húmedo
Con cielo nublado, vientos leves del sector
Noreste.
La temperatura máxima alrededor de 37º

11. What does this article inform you about?
    1. the time   3. the weather
    2. TV programs   4. business

12. What shouldn't you do today?
    1. swim   3. exercise
    2. see a movie   4. keep cool

13. To what area does this article apply?
    1. New Mexico   3. Spain
    2. Central America   4. South America

14. What is the equivalent temperature to 37º Celsius in Fahrenheit?
    1. 65º   2. 37º   3. 76º   4. 98º

Part 3b. Directions: Answer the questions based on the reading selections in Spanish. Choose the best answer to each question and write the number in the appropriate space on your answer sheet.

Regresar	Adelantar	Parar	Inicio	Recargar	Imprimir	Buscar	Finalizar

A:Juanita@pr.com ⇧
De: Isabel@ole.com
Fecha: 10 de julio-02

Querida Juanita,
Hola, estoy de vacaciones aquí en Pamplona, España durante la fiesta de San Fermín. Hace mucho calor. La temperatura es 33º C. Me gusta ver a los hombres que corren enfrente de los toros por las calles.
Hasta pronto,
Isabel

15. ¿Dónde está Isabel?
  1. Bolivia
  2. España
  3. Francia
  4. México

16. ¿Cuál es la estación del año?
  1. invierno
  2. primavera
  3. verano
  4. otoño

17. ¿Por qué está Isabel allí?
  1. Ella viaja.
  2. Ella estudia.
  3. Ella trabaja.
  4. Ella está enferma.

18. ¿Cómo es el clima?
  1. Hace calor.
  2. Hace mucho viento.
  3. Hace frío.
  4. Hace fresco.

PHYSICAL ENVIRONMENT

PART 4 WRITING (20%)

Part 4a Directions: Choose two of the three writing tasks provided below. Your answer to each of the two questions should be written entirely in Spanish and should contain a minimum of **30 words**.

Place names and brand names written in Spanish count as one word. Contractions are counted as one word. Salutations, closing, and commonly used abbreviations are included in the word count. Numbers, unless written as words, and names of people do not count as words.

Be sure that you have satisfied the purpose of the task. The sentence structure and/or expressions used should be connected logically and demonstrate a wide range of vocabulary with minimal repetition.

4a. Write a note of thirty words (30) to your friend in Madrid inviting him or her to your summer house in the country. You may wish to include:

- The name of the town
- The weather
- Physical features of the area
- The date you want him or her to visit
- The activities you can do there

4b. Write a note to your key pal in Argentina. They have the opposite seasons there, so describe how the weather and seasons are where you live.
You may wish to include:

- The name(s) and description(s) of your towns
- What the weather is like
- The type of clothing you wear
- The activities you do

4c. Your pen pal is coming to visit you this summer. Your town in Texas is by the *Río Grande*. Write a note to your pen pal describing activities that you will do during that week. You may wish to include:

- The name of the town
- The weather to expect
- The physical characteristics of the area
- The activities that you will do

PHYSICAL ENVIRONMENT

ANSWER SHEET

Nombre_____ **Fecha**_____

PART 1: SPEAKING (30%) _____
PART 2: LISTENING (30%)

                                              PART 3: READING (20%)

    2a.   2b.   2c.   3a.(8%)   3b.(12%)

1._____ 4._____   7._____   11._____   15._____

2._____ 5._____   8._____   12._____   16._____

3._____ 6._____   9._____   13._____   17._____

                       10._____   14._____   18._____

PART 4: WRITING (20%) 30 WORDS 4a , 4b or 4c Write 2 paragraphs.

1_____

_____

_____

_____

_____

_____

_____

_____

_____

2_____

_____

_____

_____

_____

_____

_____

_____

_____

PHYSICAL ENVIRONMENT

AUTHENTIC ASSESSMENT

Situation: The Wildlife Federation would like to provide environmental awareness information in many languages. Using your immediate environment, provide a model in Spanish, which could be developed as an example to Spanish-speaking teenagers.

1. Prepare a narrated video in Spanish about your immediate environment. Include plants, trees, animals, parks, other green areas, and natural geographical features. Add to this what your town is doing to conserve energy and natural resources, as well as recycling.

2. Design and label in Spanish an ideal and visually appealing natural habitat area for your town. You may draw, use magazine pictures or make use of computer graphics. Include plants, trees, and water areas that would encourage birds, butterflies and other natural wildlife that ultimately art classes could sketch and science classes could study. Add a viewing area where people could spend time admiring the natural environment. Write in Spanish a follow-up statement explaining how the habitat would change according to the weather and the seasons.

3. Some of the most beautiful artistic and literary works are written about nature. Spend time observing a plant, animal, lake, sunset or other aspect of nature. Present a visual, sound, and written expression in Spanish of your observation to the class. You might like to write a short poem in Spanish as your written expression.

4. Frequently, environmental features such as mountains, forests, beaches, etc. are important to a country for leisure, tourism or industry. Research the countries of the Hispanic world and find at least five different natural environmental features that are important to the country in which they are located. Complete the grid below based on your findings.

	País	El ambiente	La descripción	La importancia al país
1				
2				
3				
4				
5				

EARNING A LIVING

EARNING A LIVING

Las Ocupaciones:

el/la abogado,a
el/la actor,actriz
el/la artista
el/la arquitecto,a
el/la atleta
el/la bombero,a
el/la camarero,a
el/la cantante
el/la contador,a
el/la cocinero,a
el/la criado,a
el/la dentista
el/la detective
el/la diseñador,a
el/la enfermero,a
el hombre de negocios
la mujer de negocios
el/la ingeniero,a
el/la mecánico,a
el/la médico,a
el/la mesero,a
el/la modista
el/la músico,a
el/la peluquero,a
el/la periodista
el/la piloto
el/la policía
el/la profesor,a
el/la programador,a
el/la secretario,a
el/la vendedor,a
el/la veterinario,a

Más Vocabulario Relacionado:

el anuncio
la carrera
el cine
la conferencia
la compañía
el empleado,a
el empleo

la entrevista
el equipo
el futuro
el interés
el jefe
el puesto
el salario
el sueldo
la universidad

La Personalidad:

ambicioso,a
amable
independiente
inteligente
cooperativo,a
diligente

Las Actividades:

asistir a
buscar
deber
esperar
ganar
hacerse
planear
querer
recibir
trabajar
traer

Las Expresiones:

¿Qué clase de empleo quieres?
¿Qué quieres ser?
¿Cuánta experiencia tiene Ud.?
¿Dónde quiere trabajar?
¿Asiste a una universidad?
¿Qué clase de empleo prefiere?
El año que viene

EARNING A LIVING

PRE-TESTING ACTIVITIES

1. On a ditto make a list of ten occupations from the vocabulary list or from a poll taken by the students in your class. Then make ONE column for the students' signatures. Give the students 3 minutes to walk around the class asking "¿Qué quieres ser?" As they find students who desire to have the occupations on the list, they will ask for their signatures. The first 5 students who have the most signatures in the allotted time receive extra credit.

2. Divide the class into groups of 3 or 4 students (this can be done by counting off and letting all the number "ones" form a group, all the number "twos" form a group, etc.) Tell them each group represents a company. Give them 5 minutes to write an original want ad looking for an employee for their company. Then someone in each group will read the ad to the class. *As a follow-up activity for homework, the students can write an ad for themselves in which they describe themselves and the job they are seeking.

3. As a listening activity, make up 5-10 listening paragraphs in which the teacher describes the activities of a person in a certain profession. The students may select the correct answer from choices read to them or from pictures mounted on the chalk sill.

4. The students may make up business cards including logo and personal identification information.

USEFUL CULTURAL CONCEPTS FOR THIS CHAPTER

- Changing roles of women in the job market.
- NAFTA, an important economic link to Mexico.
- The euro.
- Working hours and "La siesta".
- Greater amount of vacation time, including one month of summer vacation.
- Cuban National Baseball Team

Los Refranes

- Querer es poder.
- Zapatero a tus zapatos
- Todo lo que brilla no es de oro.

EARNING A LIVING

SCHOOL-TO-WORK

A. Invite a class parent who uses Spanish in his/her work. Have students prepare questions in advance and interview the parent.

B. Invite a professor from a local college to discuss career advantages of knowing Spanish.

C. Students role-play a personnel director of a large company interviewing an applicant for a bilingual position.

SPEAKING SITUATIONS FOR PART 1 OF THE EXAM (30%)

1. You have just moved to Mexico City and are looking for a job. After reading the newspaper, you answer an interesting ad. You are now at your interview with the boss of the company.

2. You are a senior in college and are at a career goals appointment with your advisor. Tell him/her important biographical information about yourself. Mention your education and interests

3. You and your best friend are about to graduate from high school. You are discussing your goals and plans for the future.

4. Your father is a dentist and wishes you to join him in his profession. React unfavorably to this idea and indicate another profession as your choice.

EARNING A LIVING

TEACHER'S SCRIPT FOR THE EXAM, PART II (Listening, 30%)

Part 2a. Directions: For each question, you will hear some background information in English. Then you will hear a passage in Spanish twice, followed by the question in English. Listen carefully. After you have heard the question, read the question and the four suggested answers on your test paper. Choose the best answer and write its number in the appropriate space on your answer sheet.

1. Paco is listening to the radio and hears this commercial.

    Buenos días señores y señoritas. ¿No tiene buen futuro? ¿Necesita Ud. un buen empleo? Venga a una nueva compañía. Necesitamos personas ahora que hablen español e inglés.

    Who would be interested in this commercial? (2)

2. Juanita and Silvia a chatting about their plans for the future.

    -Silvia, quiero asistir a la universidad porque yo quiero hacerme profesora de inglés. Quisiera trabajar en Europa.
    -¡Ay Juanita, es fantástico.

    Why does Juanita want to attend college? (3)

3. Fernando is at an interview with his guidance counselor.

    Buenas tardes, Fernando, hoy hablamos de tus intereses para planear tu futuro. Me dices que te gusta leer y estudiar. Tú debes ir a la universidad el año que viene.

    Why did Fernando go to his counselor? (4)

Part 2b. Directions: For each question, you will hear some background information in English. Then you will hear a passage in Spanish twice, followed by the question in Spanish. Listen carefully. After you have heard the question, read the question and the four suggested answers on your test paper. Choose the best answer and write its number in the appropriate space on your answer sheet.

4. You are attending a career lecture while attending the University of Mexico.

    En esta conferencia yo voy a hablar de carreras médicas. Hay muchas posiciones hoy. Ud. puede ser enfermero, médico, veterinario o dentista. Pero es necesario estudiar en una buena universidad.

    ¿A quién le interesa esta conferencia? (1)

EARNING A LIVING

TEACHER'S SCRIPT FOR THE EXAM, PART II (Listening, 30%) Con't.

5. You are listening to the radio and hear an interview.

   Yo tengo veinte años, soy joven y bonita. Me gusta cantar y dar conciertos mucho. Tengo un disco compacto nuevo este mes.

   ¿Cuál es la carrera de esta persona? (2)

6. You are discussing summer jobs with your friend Miguel. He says

   No me gusta mi empleo para el verano. Yo trabajo doce horas al día. Yo traigo platos y limpio las mesas. No recibo mucho dinero.

   ¿Qué clase de empleo tiene Miguel.? (3)

Part 2c. Directions: For each question, you will hear some background information in English. Then you will hear a passage in Spanish twice, followed by the question in Spanish. Listen carefully. After you have heard the question, read the question and look at the four pictures on your test paper. Choose the picture that best answers the question and write its number in the appropriate space on your answer sheet.

7. You are listening to an interview on the radio.

   Me llamo José, vivo en una ciudad grande en Sudamérica. Yo soy jugador profesional de fútbol. Yo viajo por el mundo con mi equipo.

   Which picture best shows what José uses in his profession? (2)

8. Mariana has joined an organization and must describe herself. She says:

   Me llamo Mariana, yo vivo en una ciudad pequeña. Me gusta leer novelas y ayudar a la gente. Yo trabajo en una biblioteca cerca de mi casa.

   Which picture shows Mariana at work? (3)

TEACHER'S SCRIPT FOR THE EXAM, PART II (Listening, 30%)

9. You are on a bus in Madrid and overhear a man describing his profession to a friend. He says:

    Yo estudié en Francia por mucho años. Ahora yo trabajo en la Buena Mesa. Preparo platos deliciosos para mis clientes.

    Which picture best describes the occupation mentioned? (1)

10. Pepe is introducing himself to his night school class. He is mentioning his occupation as well. He says:

    Me llamo Pepe, yo corto el pelo todo el día. Me gusta hablar con mis clientes.

    Where does Pepe work? (1)

Reading Comprehension answers:

3a (8%)	11.4	12.2	13.1	14.4
3b (12%)	15.4	16.3	17.2	18.2

EARNING A LIVING

EXAMINATION

Nombre_____ Fecha_____

PART I. SPEAKING (30%)
PART 2. LISTENING (30%)

Part 2a. Directions: For each question, you will hear some background information in English. Then you will hear a passage in Spanish twice, followed by the question in English. Listen carefully. After you have heard the question, read the question and the four suggested answers on your test paper. Choose the best answer and write its number in the appropriate space on your answer sheet.

1. Who would be interested in this commercial?
   1. a child
   2. a jobless person
   3. a sick person
   4. a wealthy person

2. Why does Juanita want to attend college?
   1. to be a lawyer
   2. to be a doctor
   3. to be a teacher
   4. to be a nurse

3. Why did Fernando go to his counselor?
   1. He had a problem.
   2. He won an award.
   3. He needed a new schedule.
   4. He was planning his future.

Part 2b. Directions: For each question, you will hear some background information in English. Then you will hear a passage in Spanish twice, followed by the question in Spanish. Listen carefully. After you have heard the question, read the question and the four suggested answers on your test paper. Choose the best answer and write its number in the appropriate space on your answer sheet.

4. ¿A quién le interesa esta conferencia?
   1. a un estudiante
   2. a un pájaro
   3. a un mecánico
   4. a un piloto

5. ¿Cuál es la profesión de esta persona?
   1. Es profesora.
   2. Es cantante.
   3. Es estudiante.
   4. Es atleta.

6. ¿Qué clase de empleo tiene Miguel?
   1. Es estudiante.
   2. Es mécanico
   3. Es mesero
   4. Es atleta.

EARNING A LIVING

Part 2c. Directions: For each question, you will hear some background information in English. Then you will hear a passage in Spanish twice, followed by the question in Spanish. Listen carefully. After you have heard the question, read the question and look at the four pictures on your test paper. Choose the picture that best answers the question and write its number in the appropriate space on your answer sheet.

7.   Which picture best shows what José uses in his profession?

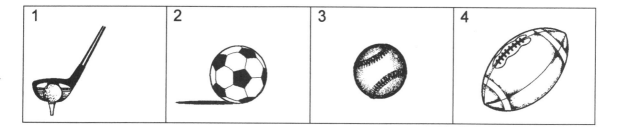

8.   Which picture shows Mariana at work

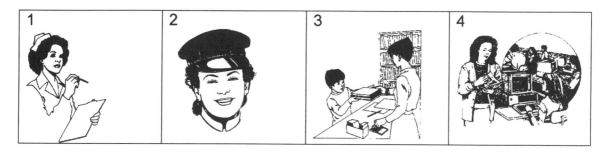

9.   Which picture best describes the occupation mentioned?

10. Where does Pepe work?

PART 3: READING (20%)

Part 3a. Directions: Answer the question in English based on the reading selection in Spanish. Choose the best answer to each question. Base your choice on the content of the reading selection. Write the number of your answer in the appropriate space on your answer sheet.

EL HOTEL MIRAMAR

Busca - un gerente
para su hotel en Panamá

Llame por una entrevista hoy. Es necesario hablar
inglés y ser organizado
Mande su curriculum vitae al Hotel Miramar,

Carretera de las Américas, 500
Panamá, Panamá

---

11. What type of job is the ad offering?
    1. secretary
    2. chambermaid
    3. bellboy
    4. manager

12. What language must the applicant speak?
    1. French
    2. English
    3. German
    4. Italian

Biografía corta

Gael García Bernal es la estrella del momento. Este hombre nació 1979, en México. Es uno de los artistas más famosos del cine mexicano. Es famoso por su interpretación en la película "Amores Perros", Está planeando comenzar la carrera de director de películas en el futuro.

---

13. What is the profession of this person?
    1. actor
    2. singer
    3. artist
    4. robber

14. What is he going to do next?
    1. drive race cars
    2. tour Mexico
    3. train dogs
    4. direct films

Part 3b. Directions: Answer the questions based on the reading selections in Spanish. Choose the best answer to each question and write the number in the appropriate space on your answer sheet.

Necesitamos

Buena Persona

Para limpiar casa,

cuidar de niños

Sueldo -$475

5 días. Dormir en casa

no necesita experiencia

llame: 555 1123

---

15. A quién le interesa este anuncio?
    1. un hombre de negocios   3. un diseñador
    2. una peluquera   4. una criada

Dra. Angela Ramos Olvera

Miembro: Colegio de Médicos del Estado de Bogotá
Miembro: Sociedad de Pediatra de Colombia
Miembro: Confederación Nacional de Pediatría

Av. Emiliano Zapata Norte 100
Santa María, Colombia
Tel. 15-46-57

9-5 lunes, martes
12-5 jueves viernes

---

16. ¿Cuál es la ocupación de esta persona?
    1. enfermera   3. médica
    2. veterinaria   4. periodista

17. Ella <u>no</u> está en su oficina el
    1. lunes   3. martes
    2. sábado   4. viernes

> **Fernando Botero**, una exposición de la obra
> de este gran pintor y escultor comienza hoy, en
> la Galería Claude Bernard, 33 East Calle 74. Inf
> 555-77-66

18. Este anuncio da información de...
    1. un autor
    2. un artista
    3. un músico
    4. un mágico

PART 4 WRITING (20%)

Part 4a Directions: Choose two of the three writing tasks provided below. Your answer to each of the two questions should be written entirely in Spanish and should contain a minimum of **30 words**.

Place names and brand names written in Spanish count as one word. Contractions are counted as one word. Salutations, closing, and commonly used abbreviations are included in the word count. Numbers, unless written as words, and names of people do not count as words.

Be sure that you have satisfied the purpose of the task. The sentence structure and/or expressions used should be connected logically and demonstrate a wide range of vocabulary with minimal repetition.

Part 4a: You have just seen an ad in a Spanish newspaper for the job of your dreams. Write a letter in Spanish applying for this job. You may wish to include:

- Why you like the job
- Your qualifications
- Previous experience
- When you can begin
- Questions you may have about the job.

Part 4b: You have just started a new summer job. Write a message to your Colombian key-pal telling him/her about your job. You may wish to include:

- Where you work
- A description of your job
- How you get to work
- Your hours and salary
- Your feelings about the job

EARNING A LIVING

Part 4c: You are interested in a part-time job after school.   You can only work on certain afternoons or on Saturday because you volunteer at the local hospital. Write a note to your guidance counselor asking for information about part-time jobs that are suitable for you. You may wish to include:

- The type of job you would like
- Your abilities
- The days and hours you can work
- The salary you want
- A request for a appointment to discuss job opportunities

EARNING A LIVING

ANSWER SHEET

Nombre_____ **Fecha**_____

PART 1: SPEAKING (30%) _____
PART 2: LISTENING (30%)   **PART 3: READING** (20%)

2a.	2b.	2c.		3a.(8%)	3b.(12%)
1._____	4._____	7._____		11._____	15._____
2._____	5._____	8._____		12._____	16._____
3._____	6._____	9._____		13._____	17._____
		10._____		14._____	18._____

PART 4: WRITING (20%) **30 WORDS   4a , 4b or 4c Write 2 paragraphs**

1_____

_____

_____

_____

_____

_____

_____

_____

_____

2_____

_____

_____

_____

_____

_____

_____

_____

_____

_____

EARNING A LIVING

AUTHENTIC ASSESSMENT

Situation: Your uncle has asked you to help him with his business. He is planning to expand his business by opening a small branch in San Juan, Puerto Rico. Use your knowledge of Spanish to help him out.

1. Choose the type of business that your uncle owns and prepare an eye-catching advertisement for a local paper. In the ad mention the name of the business, the type of service rendered, the price of the product/service, and how to make contact.

2. In order to create a wider audience, your uncle would like you to create a video to place on the Spanish language channel to tell about the business and the product. In the video show the building where the business is located, highlight the different staff members, talk about the product, and interview a satisfied customer. Use pictures from newspapers, magazines or the computer, photos, props, costumes and other people playing the different roles.

3. Having placed a help wanted ad in the local newspaper, you receive a letter from Diana Más Lopez from Santurce, Puerto Rico. Your uncle asks you to read the letter then reply to it favorably.

> Muy señor mío,
>
> Escribo esta carta para pedirle una solicitud de trabajo en su negocio. Acabo de graduarme de la universidad y quisiera trabajar para su compañía. Tengo veintidós años y soy soltera. Tengo un título en negocios y trabajé en la tienda de mi tío hace 5 años. Sé hablar inglés y español. Puedo usar la computadora. Soy responsible, amable y diligente. Le envío mi curriculum vitae también. ¿Cuál es el salario? ¿Podría trabajar tiempo parcial? ¿Cuáles son las responsabilidades del trabajo? ¿Es necesario viajar? Le agradezco por esta oportunidad. Mi teléfono es 555-98-03.
>
> Sinceramente,
>
> Diana Más López
>
> Diana Más López

LEISURE

El Cine y La Televisión:

el actor
la actriz
el anuncio
el canal
los dibujos animados
el documental
los documentarios
la estrella del cine
las noticias
la película cómica
       musical
       policíaca
       romántica
la película de ciencia ficción
       terror
       vaqueros
el programa de deportes
el reportero
las telenovelas
el televisor

Las Actividades:

acabar de
dar
durar
empezar
hacer el papel
terminar

Las Expresiones:

antes de
después de
durante
en blanco y negro
en colores

¿Quién es tu actor (actriz)
favorito(a)?

¿Cuál es tu programa de televisión
favorito?
¿Cuál es tu película favorita?
¿Qué clase de película te gusta?
¿Cuánto tiempo dura el programa?
¿A qué hora dan la película?

Los Deportes

el/la aficionado (a)
el/la atleta
el ajedrez
el asiento
el balón
el baloncesto
el básquetbol
el béisbol
el boxeo
el campo de fútbol
la corrida de toros
el dominó
la entrada
el equipo
el estadio
el esquí
el fútbol
el fútbol americano
el hockey
el (la) jugador (a)
el juego de bolos
la natación
el monopatín
el patinaje
la patineta
la pelota
la plaza de toros
el tenis
el volíbol

Las Actividades:

correr
esquiar

LEISURE

ganar
jugar
nadar
patinar
practicar
perder

enérgico,a
famoso,a
perezoso,a
variado,a

Los Adjetivos:

atlético,a

Las Expresiones:

¿Cuál es tu deporte favorito?
¿Cuál es tu equipo favorito?
¿Quién es tu jugador favorito?

PRE-TESTING ACTIVITIES

1. The teacher gives the Spanish titles of some popular movies for the class to translate. Then the students indicate what kind of movies they are.

2. The students make a survey of what kinds of movies are popular with the boys and girls in the class.

3. The students write a movie review in Spanish of a movie they have recently seen.

4. The students describe their favorite actor or actress and the roles he or she plays.

5. The students categorize sports by the seasons.

6. The students listen to a popular Spanish song on video, tape or CD. The teacher will provide the written copies of the lyrics, omitting key vocabulary words that the students should be able to recognize. Students then fill in the blanks on the sheet, supplying the missing vocabulary words as they hear the song. Compare the Spanish video seen in class with music videos of your country.

7. Each student chooses a Hispanic celebrity, such as a movie star or sports figure, and creates an eye-catching poster of the celebrity's accomplishments.

8. Have the class write individual letters or a class fan letter to Gloria Estéfan. Her address can be found at this web site: www.altocelebs.net/e/gloria-estefan/

9. Teach the students how to play "*dominó*". Then have a tournament in class. The winners can challenge the winners of the other classes.

USEFUL CULTURAL CONCEPTS FOR THIS CHAPTER

- Famous Hispanic entertainers and sports figures.
- Spanish language radio and TV programs in the United States.
- Hispanic soccer teams, *Real Madrid*
- The 1992 Summer Olympics in Barcelona
  www.cs.wustl.edu/~hba1/gymnastics/ competition/og92.html
- Cuban National Baseball Team

Los Refranes

- Dime con quien andas, y te diré quien eres
- Más vale estar solo que mal acompañado
- A caballo regalado, no le mires el diente
- Más vale tarde que nunca

SCHOOL-TO-WORK

A. Discuss how Spanish would be useful to a popular singer, opera star, ballet dancer, artist or others in entertainment, art, or sports fields. (e.g. study, perform, or compete abroad)

B. Role-play a travel agent telephoning the manager of a Hispanic hotel in order to make vacation arrangements for a client.

SPEAKING SITUATIONS FOR PART 1 OF THE EXAM (30%)

1. You are discussing television shows with your Spanish-speaking friend. Tell him what you like and why.

2. You are discussing your favorite sport with your Spanish-speaking friend. Socialize by questions, answers and comments.

3. Convince your friend to go to the movies with you this weekend.

4. Your little sister likes to watch cartoons on television. React unfavorably towards this and suggest that you both watch another channel that you would prefer.

TEACHER'S SCRIPT FOR THE EXAM, PART II (Listening, 30%)

Part 2a. Directions: For each question, you will hear some background information in English. Then you will hear a passage in Spanish twice, followed by the question in English. Listen carefully. After you have heard the question, read the question and the four suggested answers on your test paper. Choose the best answer and write its number in the appropriate space on your answer sheet.

1.   You are talking to Luis, your Spanish-speaking friend, on the phone. He says:

Hola. Leí en el periódico que hay una nueva película de terror en el cine del centro hoy. Empieza a la una en punto. Mi mamá nos llevará en carro. ¿Quieres ir conmigo?

What does Luis want to do? (4)

2.   You are watching the news on T.V. and you hear someone say this:

Muy buenas noches. Soy Ana Montalbán con el pronóstico de hoy. Ahora la temperatura está a los 80 grados. Es un buen día para la playa. Mañana va a llover por la mañana y por la tarde hará sol. Hasta luego.

What part of the news is this? (2)

3.   Carmen is telling you about her father. She says:

Mi padre es un buen atleta. Él juega al básquetbol con sus amigos en el parque todos los sábados. Los lunes juega a bolos con mi mamá. Me encantan los domingos cuando mi papá patina conmigo en la calle.

What does Carmen like to do with her father? (4)

Part 2b. Directions: For each question, you will hear some background information in English. Then you will hear a passage in Spanish twice, followed by the question in Spanish. Listen carefully. After you have heard the question, read the question and the four suggested answers on your test paper. Choose the best answer and write its number in the appropriate space on your answer sheet.

4. Julio is talking to you about his favorite T.V. show. He says:

Mi programa favorito da en el canal 3. Es la historia de una familia rica de Colombia. La actriz es muy bonita, pero tiene muchos problemas con su esposo. También su hermana tiene una enfermedad muy seria. Lo veo todos los días a las ochos de la noche. ¿Quieres verlo conmigo esta noche?

¿Qué tipo de programa es? (1)

5. Raquel is telling you about what she does after school. She says:

Mi abuela no me permite ver la tele. Ella dice que es mejor leer o jugar en el jardín. Ella piensa que no hago la tarea cuando la veo, pero siempre la hago inmediatamente cuando llego en casa. Sólo hay un televisor en casa y está en el dormitorio de mi abuela.

¿Qué hace Raquel después de las clases? (1)

6. You hear this commercial on a Spanish radio station:

Vengan al Hotel Rancho Grande y diviertánse. Tenemos todo lo que quieren para pasar una vacaciones muy buenas. Tenemos un lago, montañas, una playa grande y dos piscinas grandes para nadar, gratis, para los niños y los adultos.

¿De qué deporte habla el anuncio? (2)

Part 2c. Directions: For each question, you will hear some background information in English. Then you will hear a passage in Spanish twice, followed by the question in Spanish. Listen carefully. After you have heard the question, read the question and look at the four pictures on your test paper. Choose the picture that best answers the question and write its number in the appropriate space on your answer sheet.

7. You are talking to your friend Miguel on the phone. He says:

Vamos al parque hoy. Hay un partido de fútbol americano. Hace mucho tiempo que yo no lo juego. El partido empieza a las dos. Te veo allí. Hasta la vista.

What should you bring to the park if you want to play? (1)

8.   You are talking about your favorite movie star with your friend Carolina. She says:

Mi estrella de cine favorita tiene el pelo moreno. También es alta y bonita. Está en las películas románticas. Siempre tiene un esposo guapo. Me encantan sus películas.

Which of the following people is Carolina talking about? (1)

9.   You are listening to an interview with an actress in Spanish on the radio. She says:

Me gusta ser actriz en la televisión. No tengo un programa, pero estoy en muchos anuncios comerciales. Mi mejor anuncio fue para una tienda de ropa. Había mucha música y baile. Fue como un vídeo de rock. Llevé muchos vestidos bonitos.

What product does this actress sell? (3)

10.   You are watching a Spanish television show and you hear this announcement.

Buenas tardes. En *El Mundo de los Deportes* tenemos un torneo de bolos de los Estados Unidos. También tenemos el campeonato nacional de béisbol de Cuba. Y de Caracas tenemos una carrera de bicicletas. Regresamos dentro de un minuto.

What will you see on this program? (2)

Reading Comprehension answers:

| 3a (8%) | 11.1 | 12.4 | 13.1 | 14.3 |
| 3b (12%) | 15.2 | 16.1 | 17.2 | 18.2 |

LEISURE

Nombre_____ **Fecha**_____

EXAMINATION

PART I. SPEAKING (30%)
PART 2. LISTENING (30%)

Part 2a. Directions: For each question, you will hear some background information in English. Then you will hear a passage in Spanish twice, followed by the question in English. Listen carefully. After you have heard the question, read the question and the four suggested answers on your test paper. Choose the best answer and write its number in the appropriate space on your answer sheet.

1. What does José Luis want to do?
   1. read the newspaper
   2. watch TV
   3. drive a car
   4. go to the movies

2. What part of the news is this?
   1. sports
   2. weather
   3. entertainment
   4. world news

3. What does Carmen like to do with her father?
   1. play basketball
   2. go to the park
   3. go to the bowling alley
   4. roller skate

Part 2b. Directions: For each question, you will hear some background information in English. Then you will hear a passage in Spanish twice, followed by the question in Spanish. Listen carefully. After you have heard the question, read the question and the four suggested answers on your test paper. Choose the best answer and write its number in the appropriate space on your answer sheet.

4. ¿Qué tipo de programa es?
   1. una telenovela
   2. una comedia
   3. los dibujos animados
   4. las noticias

5. ¿Qué hace Raquel después de las clases?
   1. hace la tarea
   2. mira la televisión
   3. corre en el jardín
   4. duerme

6. ¿De que deporte hable el anuncio?
   1. el patinaje
   2. la natación
   3. el esquí
   4. el ajedrez

Part 2c. Directions: For each question, you will hear some background information in English. Then you will hear a passage in Spanish twice, followed by the question in Spanish. Listen carefully. After you have heard the question, read the question and look at the four pictures on your test paper. Choose the picture that best answers the question and write its number in the appropriate space on your answer sheet.

7. What should you bring to the park if you want to play?

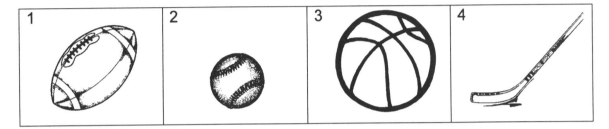

8. Which of the following people is Carolina talking about?

9. What product does this actress sell?

10. What will you see on this program?

PART 3: READING (20%)

Part 3a. Directions: Answer the questions in English based on the reading selections in Spanish. Choose the best answer to each question. Base your choice on the content of the reading selection. Write the number of your answer in the appropriate space on your answer sheet.

⬛⬛⬛⬛⬛⬛⬛⬛⬛ Guía de Ocio ⬛⬛⬛⬛⬛⬛⬛⬛⬛

(1) **El Diario de la Princesa** (EEUU) Una película cómica con Julie Andrews. Una alumna flaca y fea llega a ser princesa de un país extranjero. Vas a reírte mucho. (Cine Centro. 6.00, 8.00, 10.00)

(2) **Los Otros** (EEUU) Nicole Kidman. Una ama de casa descubre que su casa está llena de terror. Mucho miedo. (Cinemundo. 7.00 y 11.00)

(3) **I.A.:Inteligencia Artificial** (EEUU) Una película de ciencia ficción. Una pareja recibe un muchacho robot. Luego regresa su propio hijo y deja al robot solito. Un final interesante. (Cine Máximo. 9.00 y 12.00)

(4) **El Norte** (Mex) Dos hermanos salen de su casa para ir a los EEUU para una vida mejor. El resultado es fatal. Muy triste. (Cine ABC 1.00, 3.00 y 5.00)

---

11. Which movie would you go to if you wanted to see something funny?
    1. (1)   2. (2)   3.(3)   4. (4)

12. Which movie has a sad ending?
    1. (1)   2. (2)   3.(3)   4. (4)

(1)   Argentina gana la copa de tenis
(2)   El equipo nacional de Cuba pierde el partido de béisbol
(3)   EL EQUIPO DE CHILE GANA EL PARTIDO DE BEISBOL CONTRA PARAGUAY
(4)   PARTIDO FE FÚTBOL ESTA NOCHE EN EL ESTADIO AZTECA

13. What section of the newspaper would you find the above headlines?
    1. the sports section   3. The movie section
    2. the television guide   4. The business section

14. Which headline tells about a winning baseball team?
    1. (1)   2. (2)   3.(3)   4. (4)

Part 3b. Directions: Answer the questions based on the reading selections in Spanish. Choose the best answer to each question and write the number in the appropriate space on your answer sheet.

Teleguía – La guía oficial de su televisión
Martes 2
Canal Uno
7.05. **Telediario.** Noticias Nacionales
7.30. **"Hospital General"** (EEUU)
8.00. **Filmoteca** "E.T." (familia)
10.00. **Noticias Mundiales 1**
10.30. **Mundo de Tenis**
11.30. **"Clifford –El Perro Grande y Rojo"** (niños)
12.00 **La Cocina de Gloria**

15. A las diez y media, se puede ver un programa….
    1. cómico   3. de dibujos animados
    2. deportivo   4. policíaco

16. ¿A qué hora dan una película?
    1. a las ocho   3. a las siete y media
    2. a las diez   4. a las diez y media

Plaza de Valencia
Gerente: M.O. Vasquez
FERIA DE JULIO 2002
VIERNES, DÍA 31, SEIS TOROS
De la ganadería de los señores herederos de
de Madrid

Toreros
JOSÉ MARÍA MANZANAS, NIÑO DE LA CAPEA Y JOSELITO

Venta de localidades, en taquillas de la plaza, de 11 a 2 y
de 4 a 5 de la tarde. Las corridas comienzan a las 5 de la
tarde.

DIPUTACIÓN DE VALENCIA

17. ¿Para qué es este anuncio?
    1. un concierto   3. un partido de fútbol
    2. una corrida   4. una película

18. ¿A qué hora da el espectáculo?
    1. a las siete   3. a las once
    2. a las cinco   4. a las dos

PART 4: WRITING (20%)

Part 4 Directions: Choose two of the three writing tasks provided below. Your answer to each of the two questions should be written entirely in Spanish and should contain a minimum of **30 words**.

Place names and brand names written in Spanish count as one word. Contractions are counted as one word. Salutations, closing, and commonly used abbreviations are included in the word count. **Numbers, unless written as words,** and names of people do not count as words.

Be sure that you have satisfied the purpose of the task. The sentence structure and/or expressions used should be connected logically and demonstrate a wide range of vocabulary with minimal repetition.

4a. In a note to your pen pal, tell about a movie or television show that you have seen recently. You may wish to include:

- The title of the movie or TV show
- The type of movie (comedy, etc.)
- The reason you liked it
- The names of the actors in the show
- Why you do or do not recommend it

4b. In a note to your friend in Madrid, tell him about your favorite sport or athlete. You may wish to include:

- The name of the athlete or the type of sport
- Why you like it
- If and when you play the sport
- When you are going to see the athlete play
- An invitation for your friend to go to a game with you

4c. You are an exchange student in San José, Costa Rica. Write a message in Spanish to your roommate telling him or her that you went to the mall and then you have plans to go to a concert. Since you have two tickets, invite your friend to accompany you to the concert. You may wish to include:

- When you will return from the mall
- The time of the concert
- How you will get to the concert
- Who is playing at the concert
- The cost of the tickets

LEISURE

ANSWER SHEET

Nombre_____ **Fecha**_____

PART 1: SPEAKING (30%) _____
PART 2: LISTENING (30%)   **PART 3: READING** (20%)

2a.	2b.	2c.

			3a.(8%)	3b.(12%)
1.____	4.____	7.____	11.____	15.____
2.____	5.____	8.____	12.____	16.____
3.____	6.____	9.____	13.____	17.____
		10.____	14.____	18.____

PART 4: WRITING (20%) **30 WORDS** **4a , 4b or 4c Write 2 paragraphs**

1_____

_____

_____

_____

_____

_____

_____

_____

_____

2_____

_____

_____

_____

_____

_____

_____

_____

_____

_____

LEISURE

AUTHENTIC ASSESSMENT

Situation: Your Peruvian pen pal, Patricia Navarro, and her parents will soon arrive for a stay at your home. Patricia likes modern music and sports. La Señora Navarro enjoys the theater, movies and museums. El Señor Navarro is a gourmet cook and likes watching TV, reading, and sports

1. Organize the Navarro family's three-day stay with you by completing the leisure activities schedule below in accordance with each person's preferences:

Patricia:

Día	Hora	Actividad	Lugar

La Señora Navarro:

Día	Hora	Actividad	Lugar

El Señor Navarro:

Día	Hora	Actividad	Lugar

2. Using the schedule you have just planned as a reference, write a welcome note in Spanish to Patricia and her parents, summarizing in letter form what you can do together. Wish them a good trip and tell them you are waiting for their arrival.

3. To add further to your guests' interest in your planned activities, prepare a video in Spanish of yourself interviewing a famous singer, athlete, musician, movie star, author or chef. Prepare at least ten questions about the famous person's life and career. Work with a classmate who will play the role of the famous person to be interviewed. Remember, your interview should be fun and interesting to watch.

4. There are many Spanish-speaking celebrities in the entertainment, literary, art and sports fields. Select one of these people and write a report on him or her. Do your research using books, magazines, newspapers, and/or the Internet. Include interesting facts about the person's life and why he/she is famous. Share something of the person's work with your class and explain the value you find in that work.

Public and Private Services

PUBLIC AND PRIVATE SERVICES

El Teléfono

el, la telefonista
el, la operador(a)
la moneda
el número
la señal
la ranura
la llamada de larga distancia, local
la cabina del teléfono
la guía telefónica
la ficha
la tarifa

Las Actividades

hablar (por teléfono)
charlar
hacer una llamada
depositar
funcionar
comunicar
decir
marcar un número
escuchar
esperar

Las Expresiones (por el teléfono)

Aló, Bueno, Diga
¿De parte de quién?
La línea está ocupada.
temprano
Tiene el número equivocado.
¿Quién es?
Quiero (deseo) hacer una llamada.
El teléfono está descompuesto.
tarde

Las Expresiones (por el correo)

¿Cuánto vale?
¿Cuánto pesa?
¿Cuánto cuesta?
libras, onzas

El Correo

la casa de correos
el cartero, la mujer cartero
el buzón
la tarjeta postal
la dirección
la zona postal
el país
por correo aéreo
el, la empleado(a)
el sello, la estampilla
el timbre
la ventanilla
la carta
el estado
la ciudad
el paquete
el, la cliente

La Carta

el saludo
el texto
la despedida

la posdata
Querido,a
Distinguidos señores
la fecha
atentamente
un abrazo
con cariño

Las Actividades

mandar
comprar
pedir
prestar
enviar
meter
hacer cola

PUBLIC AND PRIVATE SERVICES

PRE-TESTING ACTIVITIES

1. In pairs, the students play the roles of an operator and a customer who needs assistance. The operator will ask how he/she can help the customer. The partner gives a certain name and address to be found.

2. The students sit in pairs and play the roles of post office customer and postal employee. One student needs to buy stamps and send a package. The other gives assistance. Then they may change roles.

3. The teacher brings in a telephone directory in Spanish or supplies pages from one to help the students locate numbers.

4. This may be the opportunity to start the class on letter writing. They may have pen pals in other classes or out of the state or country. They may learn salutations and closings as well as how to address an envelope. If this coincides with a holiday, an appropriate saying may be included.

USEFUL CULTURAL CONCEPTS FOR THIS CHAPTER

♦ Letter writing etiquette and forms
♦ How to make a telephone call
♦ Stamps may be purchased at *quioscos*
♦ The post office closes during *siesta* time
♦ Spanish phone numbers are made up of 6 numbers (23-65-21)

Los Refranes:

♦ Primero es la obligación que la devoción.
♦ Cada oveja con su pareja.
♦ El hombre propone y Dios dispone.
♦ El huésped y el pez, a los tres días hieden.
♦ El enfermo está lleno de buenas intenciones y el cielo de buenas obras.

SCHOOL-TO-WORK

Brainstorm with the class to create a list of professions that could make use of what is learned in this chapter. Have the students justify their answers. (Possible answers: world-wide courier service, international banker, international telephone operator, travel companion, tour guide.)

PUBLIC AND PRIVATE SERVICES

SPEAKING SITUATIONS FOR PART 1 OF THE EXAM (30%)

1. You are in Spain and have 10 postcards and a package to mail to your friends at home. Go to the post office, greet the clerk and tell him/her what you want to do. Then thank the clerk.

2. You telephone your friend. He/she is not home. Socialize with his/her sister who answers and leave a message.

3. You and your friend are having a discussion about the career you have chosen. You want to be a letter carrier and your friend wants to be a telephone operator. Convince him/her that being a telephone operator is better.

4. Your friend has moved away to Mexico. You miss him/her a lot. Call the operator and find out your friend's new number by giving the appropriate information.

TEACHER'S SCRIPT FOR THE EXAM, PART II (Listening, 30%)

Part 2a Directions: For each question, you will hear some background information in English. Then you will hear a passage in Spanish twice, followed by a question in English. Listen carefully. After you have heard the question, read the question and the four suggested answers. Choose the best answer and write its number in the appropriate space on your answer sheet (9%)

1.   You are listening to the radio in Costa Rica and hear this advertisement:

   La mejor compañía de teléfono es CRT. Tenemos precios bajos y servicio excelente. Use nuestra compañía cuando llame a su familia en otros países.

   Who should use this company?   (3)

2.   Marisol is talking about a party she is planning. She says:

   Quiero invitar a muchas personas a la fiesta el mes que viene. Necesito comprar las invitaciones. Entonces, necesito escribir las direcciones en todos los sobres.

   What must Marisol do?   (1)

3.   While in New York, Paco and his friend see a boy hit by a car. Paco says:

-Voy a llamar una ambulancia ahora mismo. ¿Cuál es el número?
-Llama 911, el número de emergencia, y da la calle donde estamos.

What is he going to do?

Part 2b Directions: For each question, you will hear some background information in English. Then you will hear a passage in Spanish twice, followed by a question in Spanish. Listen carefully. After you have heard the question, read the question and the four suggested answers. Choose the best answer and write its number in the appropriate space on your answer sheet. (9%)

4.   Manuel hears this advertisement on the radio:

¿Quieres tener más amigos? ¿Estás aburrido en casa? Llama nuestro número para hablar con muchas personas muy interesantes. No cuesta mucho: cincuenta centavos por el primer minuto.

¿Por qué debe llamar este número?   (3)

5.   There are five days before Christmas. You are at the post office and hear an employee make this announcement:

Todas las personas que van a comprar estampillas, formen una línea a la derecha del cuarto. Van a poder comprarlas más rápidamente.

¿Qué dice el empleado?   (2)

6.   You are talking with your friend Christina about your friend who is away at college.

-¿Cuál es el número de Ana en la universidad?
-No sé. Busca su número en la guía telefónica.
-Es imposible. Yo no sé el nombre de su residencia estudiantil.
-Bueno, llama a su mamá para pedir la información.

¿Cómo encuentran las chicas el número de Ana?   (4)

Part 2c Directions: For each question, you will hear some background information in English. Then you will hear a passage in Spanish twice, followed by a question in English. Listen carefully. After you have heard the question, read the question and look at the 4 pictures on your test. Choose the picture that best answers the question and write its number in the appropriate space on your answer sheet. (12%)

7. You overhear one side of a conversation on the telephone.

   ¡Diga! ¿En qué puedo sevirle? Sí, ¿Cuál es la dirección? Un momento, por favor. El número que necesita es 34 57 82. De nada.

   Who is speaking? (1)

8. You are lost in Puerto Rico and ask someone for directions.

   -Perdón señor. Puede decirme donde hay un teléfono?
   -Sí señorita. Con mucho gusto. Camine dos calles. Hay una cabina de teléfono en la esquina.

   According to the directions, what is located at the corner? (1)

9. Ramón is on vacation and is making a purchase. He says:

   -Perdón señor. Quiero comprar tarjetas postales. ¿Se venden aquí?
   -Sí señor. ¿Cuántas necesita Ud.?
   -Vamos a ver, deme diez por favor.

   What is Ramón purchasing? (4)

10. It is three weeks before Christmas, and Luis hears this public service announcement:

    Señoras y señores si Uds. van a mandar paquetes a otros países, es necesario enviarlos temprano. No espere hasta el último momento.

    To what public service does this ad refer? (1)

Reading Comprehension Answers:

3 a. (8%)	11. 2	12. 4	13. 1	14. 2
3 b. (12%)	15. 2	16. 4	17. 4	18. 1

PUBLIC AND PRIVATE SERVICES

Nombre _____   Fecha_____

EXAMINATION

Part 1 SPEAKING (30%)
Part 2 LISTENING (30%)

Part 2a Directions: For each question, you will hear some background information in English. Then you will hear a passage in Spanish twice, followed by a question in English. Listen carefully. After you have heard the question, read the question and the four suggested answers. Choose the best answer and write its number in the appropriate space on your answer sheet (9%)

1. Who should use this company?
    1. People who want to mail a package.
    2. People who are bilingual
    3. People who are calling long distance.
    4. People who are rich.

2. What must Marisol do?
    1. Write invitations.   3. Mail bills.
    2. Send postcards.   4. Make telephone calls.

3. What is he going to do?
    1. Call the operator.   3. Call his mother.
    2. Call a priest.   4. Call the emergency number.

Part 2b Directions: For each question, you will hear some background information in English. Then you will hear a passage in Spanish twice, followed by a question in Spanish. Listen carefully. After you have heard the question, read the question and the four suggested answers. Choose the best answer and write its number in the appropriate space on your answer sheet. (9%)

4. ¿Por qué debe llamar este número?
    1. para pedir dinero   3. para hablar con otra gente
    2. para un empleo   4. en caso de una emergencia

5. ¿Qué dice el empleado?
    1. Deben hacer la maleta.   3. Deben ir a casa.
    2. Deben hacer cola.   4. Deben comprar los paquetes.

6. ¿Cómo aprenden las chicas el número de Ana?
    1. Ellas llaman la telefonista.
    2. Ellas buscan el número en la guía telefónica.
    3. Ellas saben el número.
    4. Ellas llaman a su familia.

PUBLIC AND PRIVATE SERVICES

Part 2c Directions: For each question, you will hear some background information in English. Then you will hear a passage in Spanish twice, followed by a question in English. Listen carefully. After you have heard the question, read the question and look at the 4 pictures on your test. Choose the picture that best answers the question and write its number in the appropriate space on your answer sheet. (12%)

7. Who is speaking?

1.   2.   3.   4.

8. According to the directions, what is located at the corner?

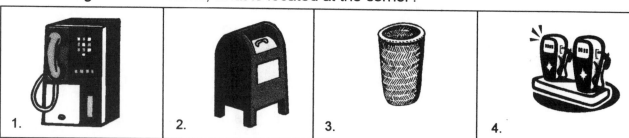

1.   2.   3.   4.

9. What is Ramón purchasing?

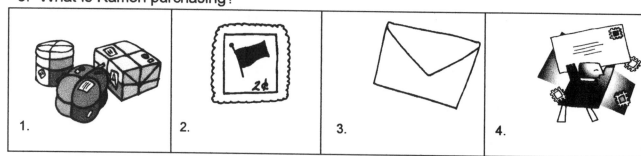

1.   2.   3.   4.

10. To what public service does this ad refer?

1.   2.   3.   4.

Part 3 READING (20%)

Part 3a Directions: Answer the questions in English based on the reading selections in Spanish. Choose the best answer to each question. Base your choice on the content of the reading selections. Write the number of your answer in the appropriate space on your answer sheet. **(8%)**

LIBROS POR CORREO

Si viven en San Joaquín, pueden hacer uso de este servicio especial para obtener libros prestados por correo. La biblioteca paga el porte! Listas de los libros que pueden ser prestados se obtienen en cualquier de las bibliotecas o llamando el número 25 37 58.

---

11. What kind of service is this?
    1. Used books are sold.
    2. Books are sent by mail.
    3. Books are discussed.
    4. Books are repaired.

12. What should you do to obtain this service?
    1. Apply in writing.
    2. Be sponsored by someone.
    3. Pay a fee.
    4. Call or go in person.

GUÍA INFORMATIVA
AREA METROPOLITANA
TELÉFONOS DE EMERGENCIA:

1. EMERGENCIA POLICÍACA	25 56 90
2. BOMBEROS	22 33 54
3. EMERGENCIA MÉDICA	22 56 89
4. CENTRO DE TRATAMIENTO DE ENVENENAMIENTO	22 14 56

---

13. Why is this list important?
    1. It contains emergency numbers.
    2. It contains restaurant numbers.
    3. It contains friends' numbers.
    4. It contains free numbers.

14. Which number would you call for the fire department?
    1. 1
    2. 2
    3. 3
    4. 4

Part 3b Directions: Answer the Spanish questions based on the reading selections in Spanish. Choose the best answer to each question. Write the number of your answer in the appropriate space on your answer sheet. (12%)

LLAMADAS INTERNACIONALES

Estas llamadas son más económicas si llaman durante las horas de la mañana y de la noche cuando llaman menos personas.

Por ejemplo: El periódo inicial de 3 minutos cuesta 35 centavos.

15. ¿De qué se trata este anuncio?
   1. precios postales   3. precios de vuelos
   2. precios telefónicas   4. precios de taxis

16. ¿Cuándo se paga menos?
   1. en las horas de negocios
   2. al mediodía
   3. el jueves
   4. temprano y tarde

LAS INSTRUCCIONES PARA HACER UNA LLAMADA:

1. Descuelgue el auricular.
2. Meta la ficha en la ranura.
3. Espere la señal.
4. Marque el número.
5. Espere la contestación.
6. Empuje el botón.
7. Empiece a hablar.

*****Este teléfono está descompuesto.*****

17. Estas instrucciones son importantes para una persona en
   1. un tren   3. un avión
   2. un barco   4. una cabina de teléfono

18. Después de depositar la ficha no hay señal, ¿por qué?
   1. El teléfono no funciona.
   2. La línea está ocupada.
   3. No hay operador.
   4. Tiene un número equivocado.

PUBLIC AND PRIVATE SERVICES

PART 4 WRITING (20%)

Part 4a Directions: Choose one of the three writing tasks provided below. Your answer to each of the two questions should be written entirely in Spanish and should contain a minimum of **30 words**.

Place names and brand names written in Spanish count as one word. Contractions are counted as one word. Salutations, closing, and commonly used abbreviations are included in the word count. Numbers, unless written as words, and names of people do not count as words.

Be sure that you have satisfied the purpose of the task. The sentence structure and/or expressions used should be connected logically and demonstrate a wide range of vocabulary with minimal repetition.

Part 4a: Your family has hired a house sitter to take care of your house while you go on vacation. The house sitter speaks Spanish. Your parents have asked you to write a note in Spanish telling the sitter how to handle the phone messages and mail. You may wish to include:

- When the mail arrives
- How to write the telephone callers' names and numbers on paper
- What to do in case of an emergency
- How to reach you

4b. You are studying for a year in Spain. You would like to send some items back home to your family. Write a note in Spanish to your host mother asking her to go to the post office for you.   You may wish to include:

- A request to go to the post office
- The items you wish to send
- How you want to send the packages
- The name and address of your parents

4c. You would like to work or volunteer at a park in your community this summer. Since you speak Spanish, you would like to work with Hispanic children. Write a note to the park director about working at the park. You may wish to include:

- Information about your abilities
- The type of job you would like
- The activities you can do with the children
- The days and hours you can work

PUBLIC AND PRIVATE SERVICES

ANSWER SHEET

Nombre_____ **Fecha**_____

PART 1: SPEAKING (30%) _____
PART 2: LISTENING (30%)

PART 3: READING (20%)

2a.	2b.	2c.
1._____	4._____	7._____
2._____	5._____	8._____
3._____	6._____	9._____
		10._____

3a.(8%)   3b.(12%)

11._____   15._____

12._____   16._____

13._____   17._____

14._____   18._____

PART 4: WRITING (20%) **30 WORDS**   **4a , 4b or 4c Write 2 paragraphs**

1_____

_____

_____

_____

_____

_____

_____

_____

_____

2_____

_____

_____

_____

_____

_____

_____

_____

_____

_____

PUBLIC AND PRIVATE SERVICES

AUTHENTIC ASSESSMENT

Getting Settled in Madrid

Situation: You and your family are spending the summer in Madrid and have just moved into an apartment in the center of Spain's capital.

1. Since your new move into your apartment, none of your mail has arrived there. Your parents think your mail is not being forwarded from your first address. Since you are studying Spanish, your parents ask you to write a note to the mailman introducing your family, explaining the problem and asking for his suggestions or help.

2. Your family has bought an answering machine. Record in Spanish your family's message. You may want to include background music to personalize the message.

3. Your Spanish teacher back home has asked you to make a demonstration video in Spanish on how the public telephone works in Spain. Using appropriate props, prepare an entertaining video for your class.

4. Having completed your video, role-play going to the Spanish post office in order to send a videotape back home to your Spanish teacher. Discuss with a postal worker the package's value, weight, destination, options for sending and cost, as well as your decision on how you will send it. A classmate will play the role of a postal worker.

5. A. Collecting post cards and stamps can be fun. Ask family and friends to lend you any postcards, stamps or greeting cards they might have from a Spanish speaking country. Do not borrow valuable items. Show them to your class and explain what you have collected. Tell what you learned from looking carefully at these items. Compare and contrast them with similar items from your country.

   B. To celebrate New Year's, Valentine's Day or other holidays, make a card in Spanish for a friend or family member. Be sure to add an appropriate message in Spanish. If there is no holiday coming up, create a decorative card and write a note in Spanish to a friend, family member or classmate.

TRAVEL

TRAVEL

Los medios de Transporte

el automóvil
el coche
la motocicleta
el camión
el barco
el tren
el carro
la bicicleta
el autobús
el taxi
el avión
el metro

El Aeropuerto y la Estación de Trenes

la puerta
la llegada
la ventanilla
el boleto (de ida y vuelta)
el horario
la tarjeta de embarque
la mochila
la maleta
el vuelo
el billete
la vía
el equipaje
el pasaporte
la salida
el asiento
el auxiliar del vuelo
la aduana
la sala de espera

El Hotel

el gerente
la escalera
la cama sencilla
la reservación
el ascensor
la habitación (individual)
             (doble)
el balneario
la cama de matrimonio
la pensión
el parador

Las Actividades

viajar
hacer un viaje
volar
sacar una foto
quedarse
hacer una reservación
subir
comprar recuerdos
ver los puntos de interés
despegar
salir de / para
manejar
llegar
ir de camping
firmar el registro
hacer la maleta
bajar
alquilar un coche
aterrizar
buscar
encontrar
planear
regatear
hacer compras
comprar
cambiar
conseguir un vuelo

TRAVEL

Otras Palabras

la casa de cambio
la oficina de turismo
la artesanía típica
los recuerdos

La Gente

el/la agente de viajes
el chófer de taxi
el/la pasajero(a)
el piloto, la mujer piloto
la azafata, el auxilar de vuelo
el/la aeromozo(a)
el/la turista
el/la aduanero(a)

Expresiones:

¿Adónde va Ud.?
¿Cuánto cuesta?
¿Cuánto tiempo se queda Ud.?
¿Cuál es la dirección?

¿Tiene Ud. una habitación?
¿De qué puerta / vía sale?
¿Cómo va Ud.?
¿Dónde queda_____?

SPANISH SPEAKING COUNTRIES

LOS PAISES QUE HABLAN ESPAÑOL

EUROPA
España
Islas Canarias

NORTEAMERICA
México

EL CARIBE
Cuba
Puerto Rico
La República Dominicana

AMERICA CENTRAL
Guatemala
El Salvador
Honduras
Nicaragua
Costa Rica
Panamá

SUDAMERICA
Colombia
Venezuela
Ecuador
Perú
Bolivia
Chile
Paraguay
Argentina

TRAVEL

PRE-TESTING ACTIVITIES

1. The students can prepare travel posters or pamphlets about different Spanish-speaking countries by using the school library, Internet or local travel agencies.

2. The students can act out a scene in a travel agency, or on an airplane or train.

3. The students can read authentic train and airline tickets and schedules, and then make their own schedule.

4. The teacher or students can prepare airline announcements as a listening comprehension. The other students can listen for the flight number, the gate number and the destination.

5. The students can make a class survey of how they prefer to travel and tabulate the results.

6. The teacher can create a virtual airplane in class by arranging desks in an airplane seat formation. Students can simulate arriving at the airplane counter and gate, entering the plane, take-off, flight, food service, landing, and customs.

USEFUL CULTURAL CONCEPTS FOR THIS CHAPTER

♦ Iberia- national Spanish airline
♦ RENFE- Spanish train
♦ AVE- fast Spanish train
♦ Aeropuerto Barajas- Madrid, Spain
♦ EURO- European currency
♦ Make students aware of the Spanish speaking countries (refer to the previous page)

Refranes:

A camino largo, paso corto.
Quien mal anda, mal acaba.

TRAVEL

SCHOOL-TO-WORK

If your school is within traveling distance to an international airport, inter-country train service or cruise line, arrange a class trip, a tour of the facility, and a meeting with an employee who uses Spanish in his/her work. If a class trip is not possible, invite a flight attendant or travel agent to class to describe his/her profession and work with Hispanic countries.

TRAVEL

SPEAKING SITUATIONS FOR PART 1 OF THE EXAM (30%)

1. It's vacation time. Your friend wants to go to Mexico City. You would rather go to a beach resort. Convince him/her to go to the beach resort.

2. You and your friend are planning to go to Miami. Go to the travel agent to plan a trip.

3. You are on an airplane going to Puerto Rico. You are seated next to someone your age. Start a conversation with him/her.

4. You and your family are planning a trip to Mexico. Your brother wants to go by car. React unfavorably to this and suggest another means of transportation.

TEACHER'S SCRIPT FOR THE EXAM, PART 2 (Listening, 30%)

Part 2a Directions: For each question, you will hear some background information in English. Then you will hear a passage in Spanish twice, followed by a question in English. Listen carefully. After you have heard the question, read the question and the four suggested answers. Choose the best answer and write its number in the appropriate space on your answer sheet (9%)

1.   You are at Barajas Airport in Madrid. You hear this announcement:

        Señores pasajeros, su atención por favor. El vuelo 50 con destino a Nueva York sale a las 10 de la puerta número 15. Gracias.

        What is the flight number? (1)

2.   You and your friend are at a train station in Bogotá, Colombia. Your friend is talking to a salesperson at the ticket window.

-¿En qué puedo sevirle?
-¿A qué hora sale el tren para Cartagena?
-Sale a las 3:15.
-Gracias. y ¿De qué vía sale?
-Sale del número 2.
-¿Cuánto cuesta un boleto?
-Cuesta 6 pesos.

What time is the train leaving for Cartagena?   (1)

3.   You hear this commercial on a Spanish language radio station:

Hola. Si Usted hace un viaje este verano, viaje Ud. con nosotros. Somos Aerolatina, y tenemos vuelos cada martes de Nueva York a Caracas a precios muy bajos durante el mes de agosto. Visite a sus parientes y a sus amigos en Sudamérica. Visítelos con nosotros!

What information have you learned according to this ad?   (2)

Part 2b Directions: For each question, you will hear some background information in English. Then you will hear a passage in Spanish twice, followed by a question in Spanish. Listen carefully. After you have heard the question, read the question and the four suggested answers. Choose the best answer and write its number in the appropriate space on your answer sheet. (9%)

4.   You are on an airplane and the pilot makes this announcement:

Buenos días. Bienvenidos señores pasajeros. Hoy vamos a Acapulco. Hace buen tiempo en Acapulco hoy. Vamos a llegar a Acapulco a las siete y media. Ahora es la una y media en Nueva York. Vamos a volar sobre Chicago hoy. Si Ud. necesita ayuda, llame a su aeromozo. Hasta la próxima.

¿Adónde va el avión?   (2)

5.   You hear this travel ad on the radio:

Venga a La Plaza Santo Domingo. Tenemos 3 piscinas y estamos cerca de la playa donde hay muchas actividades acuáticas; el wind-surf y mucho más. Visite La Plaza Santo Domingo para sus próximas vacaciones.

¿Qué es "Plaza Santo Domingo"?   (1)

TRAVEL

6. You are on vacation with your friend in Spain. You arrive at the hotel reception desk. The manager says:

Lo siento. Su reservación fue para ayer. Yo le di su habitación a otra persona. Si quiere esperar, habrá otra habitación más tarde. ¿Por qué no llamó Ud. por teléfono?

¿Cuál es el problema?   (1)

TEACHER'S SCRIPT FOR THE EXAM, PART 2 (Listening, 30%)- continued

Part 2c Directions: For each question, you will hear some background information in English. Then you will hear a passage in Spanish twice, followed by a question in English. Listen carefully. After you have heard the question, read the question and look at the 4 pictures on your test. Choose the picture that best answers the question and write its number in the appropriate space on your answer sheet. (12%)

7. You are traveling with your friend, Luis, to Los Angeles. He says:

No me gusta viajar así. El viaje es muy largo y aburrido. Siempre paramos en las estaciones y los pasajeros entran y salen. Es muy molestoso.

How are you and your friend traveling? (3)

8. You are at the airport with your friend Marta. She says:

Estoy muy preocupada. Temo que no puedo entrar en el avión. Dejé todos mis documentos en casa. Tengo que llamar a mi papá para que me los traiga aquí.

What does Marta need?   (1)

9. You and your friend, Jorge, are discussing your vacation plans. He says:

Cuando llegamos a Madrid, tomaremos el tren a Toledo. En Toledo alquilaremos unas bicicletas, para ir a Santander donde nadaremos en el mar. ¿Qué piensas?

How will you and your friend get from Toledo to Santander? (3)

10. You are at the bus station in La Paz, Bolivia, waiting for your friend Tomás to arrive. You call him on the phone. He says:

Estoy tarde porque no hice mi maleta. Toda mi ropa está en la lavandería. Tengo que esperar hasta que esté seca. Pero tengo todo el resto de mis cosas. Tengo mi billete, mi dinero, y mi cámara. Hasta pronto!

What does Jorge need?   (1)

Reading Comprehension answers:

| 3 a. (8%) | 11. 1 | 12. 3 | 13. 3 | 14. 1 |
| 3 b. (12%) | 15. 1 | 16. 4 | 17. 1 | 18. 1 |

TRAVEL

Nombre_____   **Fecha**_____

EXAMINATION

Part 1 SPEAKING (30%)
Part 2 LISTENING (30%)

Part 2a Directions: For each question, you will hear some background information in English. Then you will hear a passage in Spanish twice, followed by a question in English. Listen carefully. After you have heard the question, read the question and the four suggested answers. Choose the best answer and write its number in the appropriate space on your answer sheet (9%)

1. What is the flight number?
    1. 50
    2. 15
    3. 10
    4. 5

2. What time is the train leaving for Cartagena?
    1. 3:15
    2. 6:00
    3. 2:00
    4. 1:15

3. What information have you learned according to this ad?
    1. There are daily flights to N.Y. in the summer.
    2. There are flights to Caracas one day a week.
    3. It costs more to travel in August.
    4. Your friends can travel to New York very cheaply.

Part 2b Directions: For each question, you will hear some background information in English. Then you will hear a passage in Spanish twice, followed by a question in Spanish. Listen carefully. After you have heard the question, read the question and the four suggested answers. Choose the best answer and write its number in the appropriate space on your answer sheet. (9%)

4. ¿Adónde va el avión?
    1. Va a Chicago.
    2. Va a Acapulco.
    3. Va a New York.
    4. Va a Cancún.

5. ¿Qué es "Plaza Santo Domingo"?
    1. Es un balneario con una plaza bonita.
    2. Es un lugar en las montañas.
    3. Es el lugar para el camping.
    4. Es un parque.

6. ¿Cuál es el problema?
    1. Llegaron tarde.
    2. La habitación está sucia.
    3. El teléfono no funciona.
    4. El hotel está cerrado.

TRAVEL

Part 2c Directions: For each question, you will hear some background information in English. Then you will hear a passage in Spanish twice, followed by a question in English. Listen carefully. After you have heard the question, read the question and look at the 4 pictures on your test. Choose the picture that best answers the question and write its number in the appropriate space on your answer sheet. (12%)

7. How are you and your friend traveling?

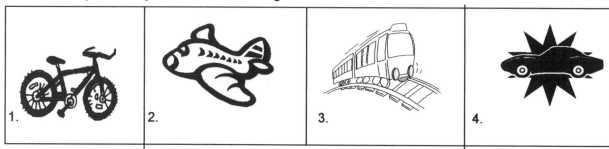

8. What does Marta need?

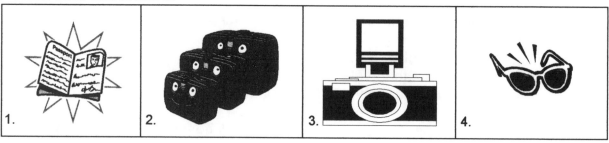

9. How will you and your friend get from Toledo to Santander?

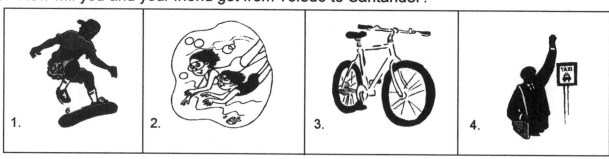

10. What does Jorge need?

Part 3 Reading (20%)

Part 3a Directions: Answer the questions in English based on the reading selections in Spanish. Choose the best answer to each question. Base your choice on the content of the reading selections. Write the number of your answer in the appropriate space on your answer sheet. **(8%)**

ESTE AGOSTO...algo grande...

ISLAS CANARIAS

Si sueñas a lo grande, con un verano inolvidable, con bellos recuerdos y temperatura ideal, ven a las Islas Canarias. Aseguramos que encontrarás algo grande: el mar, la playa, el sol y la aventura, grandes hoteles, todo a lo grande. Para un verano como en el que sueñas...Canarias te espera.

11. According to this ad, when is the best time to go to "Islas Canarias"?
    1. in the summer
    2. Christmas time
    3. for winter vacation
    4. Spring break

VACACIONES DEL REY

La familia de España, el rey Juan Carlos y su esposa, la reina Sofía, pasan sus vacaciones en Marbella, la capital del sol en la Costa del Sol en el sur de España. Pero este año viajan sin sus nietos. Los nietos de los reyes están en Paris vistando los puntos de interés.

12. How is the King of Spain spending his vacation this year?
    1. sightseeing in France
    2. working
    3. on the beach
    4. with the whole family

La Tarjeta Joven...

El nuevo servicio del RENFE, el tren nacional de España. Esta tarjeta ofrece descuentos a los jovenes entre 18 y 25 años. Viaja en segunda clase en todos los trenes. Sólo tiene que pagar un suplemento en el INTERCITY y en el TALGO. Las tarjetas son disponibles en la estación del tren en su comunidad. Traiga su certificado de nacimiento.

13. Where can you obtain the item mentioned in this ad?
    1. on the train   3. at the train station
    2. by mail   4. in a large city

14. Who can by this item?
    1. young adults   3. children
    2. anyone   4. senior citizens

Part 3b Directions: Answer the questions in English based on the reading selections in Spanish. Choose the best answer to each question. Base your choice on the content of the reading selections. Write the number of your answer in the appropriate space on your answer sheet. **(12%)**

AEROPUERTO PABLO PICASSO							
LLEGADAS				**SALIDAS**			
DE	VUELO	HORA	PUERTA	A	VUELO	HORA	PUERTA
BARCELONA	987	1000	2	MADRID	945	1205	3
VALENCIA	999	1030	4	TOLEDO	930	1130	4
TOLEDO	912	1100	1	CORDOBA	900	1115	1

15. El vuelo de Toledo aterriza....?
    1. a las once   3. en la puerta número 4
    2. a las once y media   4. a las nueve y media

16. ¿Cuál es el destino del vuelo 945?
    1. Valencia   3. la puerta número tres
    2. Barcelona   4. Madrid

AEROLATINA/ / / / / / / / / / / / / / / / /
/

Tarjeta de embarque~~~~~~~~~~~~~~~~~~~~~~~~~~~~~~

NOMBRE _____ *José Payá* _____ VUELO ___ *918* ___

DE _____ *Santiago* _____ A ___ *San Francisco* ___

ASIENTO ___ *24 D* ___ PUERTA ___ *3* ___ HORA ___ *13:15* ___

FECHA ___ *el 2 de febrero* ___ CLASE ___ *turista* ___

/ /

17. ¿Cuál es el nombre del pasajero?
    1. Payá
    2. Santiago
    3. Aerolatina
    4. Turista

18. ¿Adónde va este vuelo?
    1. Santiago
    2. San José
    3. San Francisco
    4. San Juan

TRAVEL

Part 4 Writing (20%)

Part 4a Directions: Choose two of the three writing tasks provided below. Your answer to each of the two questions should be written entirely in Spanish and should contain a minimum of **30 words**.

Place names and brand names written in Spanish count as one word. Contractions are counted as one word. Salutations, closing, and commonly used abbreviations are included in the word count. Numbers, unless written as words, and names of people do not count as words.

Be sure that you have satisfied the purpose of the task. The sentence structure and/or expressions used should be connected logically and demonstrate a wide range of vocabulary with minimal repetition.

4a: This summer you will take a trip to the country where your pen pal lives. Write a note to him or her telling about your travel plans. You may wish to include:

- A description of the place(s) you would like to visit
- The activities you are going to do there
- How you are traveling
- When you are going to visit him or her
- When you are returning home

4b: Your family is traveling to a foreign country and your parents ask you to write a note in Spanish, making the hotel arrangements. You may wish to include:

- The number of persons
- The dates of trip
- The type of room you would like
- The floor you prefer
- Special needs you may have (air conditioning, no smoking room, view)

4c. You are making plans to go to Mexico during spring break. Write a note to the tourist board asking about places to visit, hotels, and other activities to do. You may wish to include:

- The dates of your trip
- The towns you would like to visit
- Questions about the types of activities offered
- Questions about the places of interest
- Inquiries about the various hotels

TRAVEL

ANSWER SHEET

Nombre_____ **Fecha**_____

PART 1: SPEAKING (30%) _____
PART 2: LISTENING (30%)   **PART 3: READING** (20%)

2a.	2b.	2c.		3a.(8%)	3b.(12%)
1._____	4._____	7._____		11._____	15._____
2._____	5._____	8._____		12._____	16._____
3._____	6._____	9._____		13._____	17._____
		10._____		14._____	18._____

PART 4: WRITING (20%) **30 WORDS   4a , 4b or 4c Write 2 paragraphs**

1_____

_____

_____

_____

_____

_____

_____

_____

_____

2_____

_____

_____

_____

_____

_____

_____

_____

_____

_____

TRAVEL

AUTHENTIC ASSESSMENT

Enjoying a New Adventure

Situation: As a bonus for having spent this year studying Spanish, you are being rewarded with a dream vacation anywhere in the Spanish speaking world that is of interest to you.

1. Choose any Hispanic country that attracts your interest. Be adventuresome. Research this country using books, magazine articles, interviews, brochures, and/or the Internet. Make a travel log for your trip in which you include:

   A. A map of the country indicating the path of your itinerary which should contain one major city, places of historical and cultural interest, as well as other areas for which the country is famous.

   B. Complete the following questionnaire. Base your answers on your research and interests.

MI VIAJE A UN PAIS HISPANO

PAIS: _____

Ciudad principal: _____

Cinco puntos de interés en la ciudad:	Razón por mi selección:
1.	
2.	
3.	
4.	
5.	

Tres puntos de interés afuera de la ciudad:	Razón por mi selección:
1.	
2.	
3.	

AUTHENTIC ASSESSMENT- continued

C. Los medios de transporte:

    1. para ir de mi casa al país seleccionado: _____

    2. para recorrer el país: _____

D. Los regalos:

    1. Una cosa típica del país que me gustaría para decorar mi dormitorio es:

    _____

    2. Otro objeto de artesanía del país que he escogido para mi familia es:

    _____

    y para mi mejor amigo(a)?

    _____

E. Una comida del país que deseo probar:

    _____

F. Después de un año escolar en este país, estas son mis actividades favoritas para me gozar y relajar:

    _____

G. **Las preparaciones:**

Esta es una lista de cinco cosas que traigo en este viaje con la excepción

de ropa:

    1. _____

    2. _____

    3. _____

    4. _____

    5. _____

AUTHENTIC ASSESSMENT- continued

2. It is advisable to reserve hotel accommodations in advance. Role-play a conversation in Spanish with a classmate in which you telephone from your home to a hotel in a country you plan to visit. Give the details of the type of room you prefer, ask about the hotel facilities, inquire about price, and reserve a room. Role-play this situation in class or record it on audio tape.

3. Imagine the best possible day during your trip. It is a perfect day you want to remember forever. Relive the day's events by writing about that day in Spanish from start to finish in your journal. If you prefer, you can write this in the form of an e-mail message to a friend. Write approximately 75 words.

4. It's time to return home. You hurry into a store and choose a bumper sticker to remind yourself of the area you saw: region, city, monument, or other attractions. Using drawings, magazine pictures, paper cut-outs, and/or computer graphics, design the bumper sticker. Indicate the name of the place, plus give an eye-catching pictorial representation of it. Include a slogan or descriptive words in Spanish.

5. **CompartImos!**

   A. Share your dream trip with your classmates by giving an oral account of your travel adventure. Contribute your bumper sticker to a class display of other Hispanic bumper stickers made by your classmates. This display may be placed on the class bulletin board, in the school library or school display case.

   B. Keep a record of other Hispanic vacation areas. Complete the grid on the next pages as your classmates share the vacation of their dreams with the class.

TRAVEL-AUTHENTIC ASSESSMENT- continued

Nombre de estudiante: _____ País de su viaje:_____

Ciudad principal:_____

Tres puntos de interés :
1. _____

2. _____

3. _____

La información del país: ___excelente ___muy bien ___bien ___pobre

---

Nombre de estudiante: _____ País de su viaje:_____

Ciudad principal:_____

Tres puntos de interés :
1. _____

2. _____

3. _____

La información del país: ___excelente ___muy bien ___bien ___pobre

---

Nombre de estudiante: _____ País de su viaje:_____

Ciudad principal:_____

Tres puntos de interés :
1. _____

2. _____

3. _____

La información del país: ___excelente ___muy bien ___bien ___pobre

---

TRAVEL

Nombre de estudiante:_____ País de su viaje:_____

Ciudad principal:_____

Tres puntos de interés :
1. _____

2. _____

3. _____

La información del país: ___excelente ___muy bien ___bien ___pobre

---

Nombre de estudiante:_____ País de su viaje:_____

Ciudad principal:_____

Tres puntos de interés :
4. _____

5. _____

6. _____

La información del país: ___excelente ___muy bien ___bien ___pobre

---

Nombre de estudiante:_____ País de su viaje:_____

Ciudad principal:_____

Tres puntos de interés :
7. _____

8. _____

9. _____

La información del país: ___excelente ___muy bien ___bien ___pobre

Final Examination

FINAL EXAMINATION

CHECKPOINT A

TEACHER'S SCRIPT

PART 1   SPEAKING   30%

SOCIALIZING:

1. (Teacher initiates) I am a friend. I will begin the conversation by inviting you to my house. You will accept, and then we will talk about what we will do.

2. (Teacher initiates) I am a new student in you Spanish class. I will start by introducing myself, and then we will talk about ourselves.

3. (Student initiates) You are a passenger on an airplane. I am sitting next to you. Start the conversation by introducing yourself. Then try to get me to talk about the purpose of my trip.

4. (Teacher initiates) I am your cousin from Peru and you are spending the summer at my house. We are discussing activities that we might do. I will start by telling you what we could do.

5. (Student initiates) I am your friend. We are talking about going to the park for the afternoon.   Let's discuss the details of the outing. You start by making a suggestion.

6. (Teacher initiates) I am a friend. I see you in a shopping center. I greet you and I start a conversation. Then we will talk about the things we want to buy.

7. (Student initiates) I am your friend. We are discussing the gift that I have just given to you for your birthday. You start the conversation.

8. (Student initiates) I am a visiting student from Venezuela. You will ask me about my country, and I will ask about yours.

9. (Teacher initiates) I am a friend. We are making plans to see a movie this afternoon. We are discussing the details. I will start the conversation.

10. (Student initiates) I am your former Spanish teacher. You see me at school on the last day. We discuss your plans for the summer. You will start the conversation.

FINAL EXAMINATION

PROVIDING AND OBTAINING INFORMATION

1. (Student initiates) I am your friend. We are making plans to go to a soccer game this afternoon. Discuss the details. You start the conversation.

2. (Student initiates) You have a very sore throat. You stop by the doctor's office to make an appointment. I am the receptionist. You start the conversation.

3. (Teacher initiates) You are in a clothing store. I am the salesperson. I will start the conversation by finding out how I can help you.

4. (Student initiates) I am your friend from Mexico. You will be visiting Mexico soon. You want me to give you some ideas for things to do on your trip. You start the conversation.

5. (Teacher initiates) I am your teacher. Your pen pal from Argentina is coming to visit you. You tell me about your friend. I will start the conversation.

6. (Teacher initiates) You are looking for a new house. I am a real estate agent. I will begin the conversation by asking how I may help you.

7. (Student initiates) I am an exchange student who has just arrived in your town from Madrid, Spain. I want to know all about your town. You start the conversation.

8. (Teacher initiates) I am your friend. We are planning to have a graduation party. We must agree on the details. I will start the conversation.

9. (Student initiates) I am your friend. You see me in the nurse's office in school. You will begin the conversation by asking how I am, then we will continue speaking.

10. (Student initiates) I am a vendor at an open-air market in Chile. You want my advice about what fruit and vegetables to buy. You will start the conversation.

FINAL EXAMINATION

PERSUASION

1. (Student initiates) I am a friend. We just saw a basketball game. I want to go home because I have to study for a test. Try to convince me to do something else with you. You start the conversation.

2. (Student initiates) Your class is on a bus returning from seeing a Spanish play. I am your teacher. Try to convince me to stop at a restaurant. You start the conversation.

3. (Teacher initiates) I am one of your friends. We are planning an outing to the beach. I want to go to a pool. Try to convince me to have the outing somewhere else. I will start the conversation.

4. (Teacher initiates) I am your friend, and we are going out to dinner. I will start by telling you where we should go. You try to convince me to go somewhere else.

5. (Teacher initiates)   I am a friend. There is a soccer game this afternoon. I will start the conversation by telling you that I do not want to go. Try to convince me to go with you.

6. (Teacher initiates)   I am your friend. I want to go to the bull fight today, but you want to go shopping. Try to convince me to go shopping with you. I will start the conversation.

7. (Student initiates) I am a salesclerk who sold you a jacket. Try to convince me to let you exchange it for another. You start the conversation.

8. (Teacher initiates)   I am your Spanish teacher. I will begin by telling you there is a test tomorrow. You will try to convince me to postpone it.

9. (Teacher initiates)   I am a friend. I am going to suggest that we go out to a restaurant for dinner. You are not very hungry, and you will try to convince me to go somewhere else for ice cream.

10. (Teacher initiates)   I am your classmate. We have an important test tomorrow. I will start the conversation by telling you that I still intend to go to the baseball game and don't intend to study. You try to talk me out of it.

FINAL EXAMINATION

EXPRESSING FEELINGS

1. (Teacher initiates)   I am your teacher. You are leaving this school. You will be attending another school. Tell me how your feel about this change. I will begin the conversation.

2. (Student initiates) I am your friend. You have just received your class schedule. It is not what you expected. Tell me how you feel about it. You start the conversation.

3. (Teacher initiates)   I am your friend. I will start the conversation by telling you what kind of food I like. Then we will talk about what kind of food you prefer.

4. (Teacher initiates)   I am your friend, and while we are watching a show it ends. I want to watch a baseball game next. You prefer to watch a movie because you hate watching sports on TV. Express your feelings.

5. (Teacher initiates)   I am a foreign student in your class. I will tell you what I like about your country. You give me your opinion. I will start the conversation.

6. (Student initiates) I am your friend. We have plans to go to the movies tonight. We can't agree on the kind of movie to see. I prefer mysteries. Begin the conversation by expressing your opinion.

7. (Teacher initiates)   I am doing a survey to find out about the favorite television programs of American teenagers. I will start by asking you what your favorite program is. Then we will discuss it.

8. (Teacher initiates)   I am your friend. I will ask you to see a movie with me, but you have already seen it. Give me your opinion of the movie. I will start the conversation.

9. (Teacher initiates)   You are shopping for a gift for your grandmother. I am the sales clerk, and I will start the conversation by suggesting a particular gift. Then we will discuss the selection.

10. (Teacher initiates)   I am a classmate. We are talking about our new Spanish teacher. I will start the conversation.

FINAL EXAMINATION

PART 2 LISTENING 40%

TEACHER"S SCRIPT FOR PART 2 (LISTENING) OF THE EXAM (40%)

Part 2a Directions: For each question, you will hear some background information in English. Then you will hear a passage in Spanish twice, followed by the question in English. Listen carefully. After you have heard the question, read the question and the four suggested answers. Choose the best answer and write its number in the appropriate space on your answer sheet.

1. You are listening to the radio and hear this advertisement.

    Atención, por favor. ¡Hay una venta extraordinaria hoy! Hay sillas, mesas, camas, y toda clase de muebles para su casa. ¡Venga hoy y ahorre mucho!

    Why should you go to this store? (4)

2. You are at school, and your teacher is talking to your friend Luis. She says:

    Vamos a empezar la lección de matemáticas. Luis, ve a la pizarra, toma la tiza, y escribe estos números por favor.

    What must Luis do? (3)

3. Your mother is speaking to your father about the purchase of a new home. She says:

    Me gusta esa casa mucho. Es grande con una sala enorme y un comedor gigantesca. Hay cuatro dormitorios y un garaje para tres coches. Cada niño tiene su propio cuarto. También hay tres cuartos de baño.

    Why does your mother want to buy this house? (3)

4. While the Smith family is on vacation in Mexico, a guide tells them about a tradition practiced there. He says:

    Durante el mes de diciembre, todos los niños están alegres porque es la Navidad. Hay una procesión de las posadas por las calles. Entonces los niños rompen una piñata en el patio de uno de sus vecinos.

    What holiday is he describing? (1)

5. Your family is on a trip to visit your cousin Amelia. You mother is describing where she lives.

Amelia no vive en un pueblo pequeño. Hay edificios viejos y rascacielos muy altos. Los peatones y el tráfico van rápidamente por las avenidas y los bulevares. Es necesario tener cuidado al cruzar la calle.

Where do you expect to be going? (2)

6. You are traveling and hear this announcement.

Atención, pasajeros del vuelo número 123. Aborden todos Uds. el avión ahora mismo. Vamos a despegar dentro de diez minutos. Este es el último anuncio antes de salir.

What should you do? (3)

7. It is vacation time. Pablo and his friends are discussing their pastimes. He says:

Durante el verano me gusta ir a la playa y a la piscina. Estoy en el agua cada día. A veces, vamos al lago para pescar y nadar. Yo paso muchas horas en mi barco pequeño.

What does Pablo like to do best? (4)

8. You are listening to the radio and hear this advertisement.

Buenos diás, señoras y señores. Hay una ganga fantástica al Almacén Flores. Tenemos vestidos, dos por cinco mil pesos. Los pantalones para caballeros, tres por 10 mil pesos. El sábado cerramos las puertas a las once de la noche. No se olviden. ¡Es fabuloso!

What should you do? (3)

9. You are in a restaurant, and the waiter is talking to you. He says:

    Buenas noches señores. Esta noche la especialidad del día es la paella valenciana que tiene el arroz, los mariscos, las salchichas, el pollo y los tomates. También, con este plato Ud. recibe una ensalada mixta y gazpacho. El postre no está incluído.

    What does the waiter recommend? (3)

10. You are in Madrid walking down the Ramblas with your friend. Someone yells out:

    ¡Tenga cuidado! ¡No cruce! La luz está roja. Espere la luz verde.

    What should you do? (4)

Part 2b Directions: For each question, you will hear some background information in English. Then you will hear a passage in Spanish twice, followed by the question in Spanish. Listen carefully. After you have heard the question, read the question and the four suggested answers on your test paper. Choose the best answer and write its number in the appropriate space on your answer sheet.

11. You are listening to the radio and hear this interview.

    Soy alto, tengo seis pies, cinco pulgadas. Peso ciento cincuenta libras. Me llaman el Príncipe del Fútbol porque meto muchos goles para mi equipo, Los Astros de Miami.

    ¿Qué carrera tiene este hombre? (2)

12. While driving in a car in Mexico, you hear this announcement.

    Hay una epidemia del abuso de las drogas en este país. El remedio empieza con la juventud. Diga "no" a las drogas y "sí" al resto de su vida.

    ¿Cuál es el aviso de este anuncio? (4)

13. While on vacation, you go to the post office. You speak to an employee.

Perdón, señor. Yo quiero enviar este paquete a los Estados Unidos. También, deseo comprar veinte estampillas. ¿Cuánto le debo?

¿Qué vas a hacer entonces? (1)

14. You are driving on a highway in Spain and stop to ask directions to Santiago de Compostela. A pedestrian says:

Buenos días. La ciudad de Santiago está muy lejos de aquí. Tiene que seguir esta carretera por ochenta millas; pero hay curvas peligrosas y no puede ir muy rápido.

¿Qué debes hacer? (1)

15. You hear the ad on the radio.

Si tú eres aficionado a las telenovelas, este servicio es muy importante para tí. Llámanos para saber lo que pasa con tus personajes favoritos. Llama ahora. Es muy barato. Cobramos cincuenta centavos por tres minutos.

¿Qué servicio ofrece este anuncio? (2)

Part 2c Directions: For each question, you will hear some background information in English. Then you will hear a passage in Spanish twice, followed by the question in English. Listen carefully. After you have heard the question, read the question and look at the four pictures in your test. Choose the picture that best answers the question and write its number in the appropriate space on your answer sheet.

16. You are listening to a weather report on the radio and you hear this:

No hace buen tiempo hoy. Hace frío y llueve mucho. Hay una posibilidad de lluvia mañana. No veremos el sol hasta el jueves.

What is the weather? (4)

17. Ana is talking about a relative who is coming to visit. She says:

Mi primo Paco vive en Chile. Es muy alto y atlético. Visita con nosotros durante el verano. El tiene veinte años y es muy guapo. El estudia medicina y asiste a la Universidad de Salamanca en España.

Who is the person being described? (1)

18. You are talking with your friend about your activities. He says:

Durante los meses cuando hay clases, yo estudio mucho en mi dormitorio. Tengo mucha tarea y muchos proyectos, especialmente en la clase de estudios sociales. Tengo un escritorio grande con una computadora. ¡Ay de mí! Tengo un examen mañana. ¡Adios!

What is he going to do now? (2)

19. The children are getting ready to leave the house. Mother says:

Son las siete y media. El autobús viene a las ocho menos cuarto. Coman el desayuno rápidamente. Entonces, cepíllense los dientes y vayan a la parada del autobús. Lleven sus libros y la tarea.

Where are the children going? (1)

20. Enrique and his friends are deciding where to go this afternoon. Enrique says:

--Paco, ¿Adónde quieres ir esta tarde después de las clases?
--Enrique, yo quiero ir al centro para comprar un regalo para Marco. Su cumpleaños es el sábado. Voy a comprarle unos guantes.
--Muy bien. Yo necesito una chaqueta nueva, también.

Where did the friends decide to go? (3)

Reading Comprehension answers:

3a (8%)	21 __3__	22 __2__	23 __4__	24 __2__
3b (12%)	25 __2__	26 __4__	27 __2__	28 __3__
	29 __2__	30 __2__		

FINAL EXAMINATION

Nombre_____ la fecha_____

PART 1 SPEAKING (30%)
PART 2 LISTENING (40%)

Part 2a Directions: For each question, you will hear some background information in English. Then you will hear a passage in Spanish twice, followed by the question in English. Listen carefully. After you have heard the question, read the question and the four suggested answers. Choose the best answer and write its number in the appropriate space on your answer sheet.

1. Why should you go to the store?
    1. They are going out of business.
    2. They are having a sale on clothing.
    3. They are having a contest.
    4. They are having a sale on furniture.

2. What must Luis do?
    1. sing   3. write
    2. study   4. read

3. Why does your mother want to buy this house?
    1. It is not expensive.
    2. It is the only one for sale.
    3. It is the right size.
    4. It is the right color.

4. What holiday is he describing?
    1. Christmas   3. Thanksgiving
    2. Columbus Day   4. Easter

5. Where do you expect to be going?
    1. to a small town   3. to the mountains
    2. to the city   4. to the beach

6. What should you do?
    1. Buy a ticket.   3. Enter the plane.
    2. Board the train.   4. Take your seat on the bus.

7. What does Pablo like to do best?
    1. skate   3. ski
    2. play basketball   4. swim

8. What should you do?
    1. Buy flowers.   3. Shop at the store.
    2. Lock up at 11 pm.   4. Eat at the restaurant.

9. What does the waiter recommend?
    1. a drink
    2. a steak
    3. the special dish
    4. the lobster dinner

10. What should you do?
    1. Look both ways.
    2. Do not enter.
    3. Merge.
    4. Obey the traffic light.

Part 2b Directions: For each question, you will hear some background information in English. Then you will hear a passage in Spanish twice, followed by the question in Spanish. Listen carefully. After you have heard the question, read the question and the four suggested answers on your test paper. Choose the best answer and write its number in the appropriate space on your answer sheet.

11. ¿Qué carrera tiene este hombre?
    1. mecánico
    2. atleta
    3. profesor
    4. policía

12. ¿Cuál es el aviso de este anuncio?
    1. Tome vitaminas.
    2. No use aspirinas.
    3. No tome medicina.
    4. No use substancias ilegales.

13. ¿Qué vas a hacer entonces?
    1. pagar la cuenta
    2. comer la comida
    3. salir de la tienda
    4. recibir dinero

14. ¿Qué debes hacer?
    1. Manejar con cuidado.
    2. Llamar la policía.
    3. Manejar rápidamente.
    4. Regresar a casa.

15. ¿Qué servicio ofrece este anuncio?
    1. información sobre el tiempo.
    2. información sobre programas de televisión.
    3. información sobre los deportes.
    4. la hora exacta.

Part 2c Directions: For each question, you will hear some background information in English. Then you will hear a passage in Spanish twice, followed by the question in English. Listen carefully. After you have heard the question, read the question and look at the four pictures in your test. Choose the picture that best answers the question and write its number in the appropriate space on your answer sheet.

16. What is the weather?

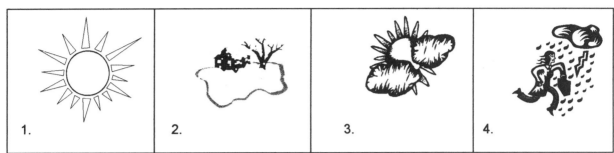

17. Who is the person being described?

18. What is he going to do now?

19. Where are the children going?

20. Where did the friends decide to go?

PART 3 READING (20%)

Part 3a Directions: Answer the English questions based on reading selections in Spanish. Choose the best answer to each question. Base your choice on the content of the reading selection. Write the number of your answer in the appropriate space on your answer sheet. (8%)

TARJETA TURÍSTICA

O RENFE

1. ESPAÑA   *153 -*

                         2. PRECIO

  Madrid   *15/8/03*
3. DESTINO   4. PRIMER DÍA VÁLIDO

  Karen Green
5. NOMBRE Y APELLIDO
    076243161
6. NÚMERO DE PASAPORTE
          LOS ESTADOS UNIDOS
7. PAÍS

---

21. This card would be used for
    1. purchasing food   3. travel
    2. renting a car   4. entering a hospital

22. Which line contains the person´s country of origin?
    1. 1   3. 5
    2. 7   4. 2

SECRETARIA DE EDUCACIÓN PÚBLICA
Dirección General De Educación Media

La Subdirección de la Escuela Secundaria Colegio Puertorriqueño de Niñas, pertenece al Sistema Educativo Nacional certifica: que según constancias que obran en el archivo, la alumna

Olga Nuñez

Cursó las materias de CICLO DE EDUCACIÓN SECUNDARIA que a continuación se expresan con las calificaciones finales que se anotan:

PRIMER GRADO	HORAS SEMANALES	CALIFICACIONES
Español	4	70
Análisis Matemático	3	75
Biología	4	70
Geografía	3	75
Historia	4	65
Lengua Extranjera - Ingés	3	80
ACTIVIDADES		
Educación Cívica	2	80
Tecnológia	2	70
Educación Física	2	70

23. For what level of education is this report card given?
    1. elementary school
    3. nursery school
    2. college
    4. high school

24. According to these grades, which subject should she study more?
    1. English
    3. Math
    2. History
    4. Geography

105.9 AM

RADIO EDUCACIONAL

Le Presenta:

Hora		Programa	Días
5:30	(1)	NOTICIERO	DE LUNES A VIERNES
6:00	(2)	ALREDEDOR DEL MUNDO EN INGLÉS	MIÉRCOLES
7:30	(3)	LOS GRANDES DE LA MÚSICA MEXICANA	DE LUNES A MARTES
8:00	(4)	MUNDO DEPORTE	DE LUNES A VIERNES

---

25. Which program will help someone who is learning English?
    1. 1   3. 3
    2. 2   4. 4

26. Which program would you listen to if you were interested in sports?
    1. 1   3. 3
    2. 2   4. 4

Part 3b Directions: Answer the Spanish questions based on reading selections in Spanish. Choose the best answer to each question. Base your choice on the content of the reading selection. Write the number of your answer in the appropriate space on your answer sheet. (12%)

1

FIESTA DE LA JUVENTUD

El sábado 22, durante todo el día, el pueblo de Alcalá celebra la Fiesta de la Junventud en la Mancomunidad Intermunicipal de Sudeste de nuestra región. Se alternan entre el pueblo y una playa; exhibiciones, competencias de deportes, juegos tradicionales y más. Todas las actividades son de participación libre y gratuita. Todos los jóvenes entre 6 y 18 pueden participar.

27. ¿Para quiénes es esta fiesta?
    1. los viejos
    2. los niños
    3. los profesores
    4. los artistas

28. ¿Qué clase de actividades hay?
    1. literarias
    2. artísticas
    3. deportivas
    4. de artisanías

¡VALENCIA SUR!

En Valencia Sur se edifican ahora 4.345 nuevas viviendas. No es sólo un proyecto de edificación residencial. Hay también: parques y espacios públicos, centros recreativos servicios y áreas comerciales que se convertirán Valencia Sur en un barrio cálido y habitable desde el primer momento.

VALENCIA SUR

El Consorcio Urbanístico Valencia Sur Está integrado por: El Instituto de la Vivienda de Valencia, La Sociedad Estatal SVG y La Empresa Municipal de la Vivienda Del Ayuntamiento de Madrid.

---

29. Este anuncio es importante si quiere
    1. comprar una casa
    2. viajar a Valencia
    3. estudiar las costumbres de Valencia
    4. asistir a la Universidad de Valencia

30. ¿Qué se ofrece?
    1. un viaje gratis
    2. una buena vecindad
    3. una famosa universidad
    4. un museo extraordinario

PART 4 WRITING (20%)

Part 4a Directions: Choose **two** of the three writing tasks provided below. Your answer to each of the two questions should be written entirely in Spanish and should contain a minimum of **30 words**.

Place names and brand names written in Spanish count as one word. Contractions are counted as one word. Salutations, closing, and commonly used abbreviations are included in the word count. Numbers, unless written as words, and names of people do not count as words.

Be sure that you have satisfied the purpose of the task. The sentence structure and/or expressions used should be connected logically and demonstrate a wide range of vocabulary with minimal repetition.

4a. You and your friend had plans to go to the mall this afternoon. You are at your friend's house but he is not home. Write him a note telling him your plans. You may wish to include:

- The time you were at his house
- Where you are going
- Why you are going
- With whom you are going
- Where you are going to be later
- Activities you can do together

4b. You have a "key pal" in Mexico. Write an e-mail message in Spanish to your Mexican key pal telling him or her about your neighborhood. You may wish to include:

- The name(s) and description(s) of the place(s)
- Where you like to go
- With whom you go
- Why you go there
- When you go there

4c. You are visiting your pen pal in Barcelona, Spain this summer. Write a postcard to your family telling about your visit. You may wish to include:

- The name of the town
- The activities you are doing
- A description of the family
- Information about the house
- The weather
- The food you are eating

ANSWER SHEET

Nombre y Apellido _____ Fecha _____

Part I   **Speaking** _____ (30%)

Part 2   **Listening (40%)**

2a   1 _____   2 _____   3 _____ 4 _____   5 _____

        6 _____   7 _____   8 _____   9 _____   10 _____

2b   11 _____   12 _____   13 _____ 14 _____ 15 _____

2c   16 _____   17 _____ 18 _____ 19 _____ 20 _____

Part 3   **Reading (20%)**

3a   21 _____ 22 _____ 23 _____

3b   24 _____ 25 _____ 26 _____

3c   27 _____   28 _____ 29 _____ 30 _____

Part 4   **Writing (10%) 30 words**
               4a , 4b, or 4c

1._____

_____

_____

_____

_____

_____

_____
_____
_____
_____
_____
_____
_____

2._____
_____
_____
_____
_____
_____
_____
_____
_____
_____
_____
_____
_____
_____
_____
_____
_____
_____
_____
_____